Getting to Know Vue.js

Learn to Build Single Page Applications in Vue from Scratch

Brett Nelson

Apress®

Getting to Know Vue.js

Brett Nelson
Eagan, Minnesota, USA

ISBN-13 (pbk): 978-1-4842-3780-9　　　　　ISBN-13 (electronic): 978-1-4842-3781-6
https://doi.org/10.1007/978-1-4842-3781-6

Library of Congress Control Number: 2018955705

Managing Director, Apress Media LLC: Welmoed Spahr
Acquisitions Editor: Jade Scard
Development Editor: James Markham
Coordinating Editor: Nancy Chen

Cover designed by eStudioCalamar

Cover image designed by Freepik (www.freepik.com)

Distributed to the book trade worldwide by Springer Science+Business Media New York, 233 Spring Street, 6th Floor, New York, NY 10013. Phone 1-800-SPRINGER, fax (201) 348-4505, e-mail orders-ny@springer-sbm.com, or visit www.springeronline.com. Apress Media, LLC is a California LLC and the sole member (owner) is Springer Science + Business Media Finance Inc (SSBM Finance Inc). SSBM Finance Inc is a **Delaware** corporation.

For information on translations, please e-mail rights@apress.com, or visit http://www.apress.com/rights-permissions.

Apress titles may be purchased in bulk for academic, corporate, or promotional use. eBook versions and licenses are also available for most titles. For more information, reference our Print and eBook Bulk Sales web page at http://www.apress.com/bulk-sales.

Any source code or other supplementary material referenced by the author in this book is available to readers on GitHub via the book's product page, located at www.apress.com/9781484237809. For more detailed information, please visit http://www.apress.com/source-code.

Printed on acid-free paper

For Danielle

Table of Contents

About the Author

Brett Nelson is a software developer who has been working with Salesforce.com since early 2016. Brett is a consultant with Just Some Apps, www.JustSomeApps.com. Prior to working in the Salesforce-land, Brett spent four years working with the .NET technology stack, focusing on web development with MVC, Angular, TypeScript, and Aurelia.

Beyond the technology, Brett is passionate about continuous improvement through learning, sharing with others, and collaboration amongst the geek society.

You can read Brett's ramblings at WIPDeveloper.com and follow him on Twitter @BrettMN.

About the Technical Reviewer

Toby Jee is a software programmer currently located in Sydney, Australia. He loves Linux and open source projects. He programs mainly in Java, JavaScript, TypeScript, and Python. In his spare time, Toby enjoys walkabouts, reading, and playing guitar.

CHAPTER 1

Why Vue.js?

Getting started with a new JavaScript framework can be a difficult task to approach. To help with this, we will take a look at the value that Vue.js brings to development and create our first app with Vue.

The Value of Vue.js

Getting started creating a Single Page Application (SPA) can be a difficult task. There are a lot of choices that have to be made up front with most frameworks. Some frameworks make those choices for you when you decide to go with them. Others require you to make those choices. Either way, those choices probably need to be decided at the beginning of a project, since changing them later in the development process will incur a greater cost.

It's a lot to process and decide, all before you do any "real" work that can you can show to your boss/client/stakeholder that they will perceive as valuable. What's a developer to do?

One option is to choose a preset way to build your SPA that someone else had some luck with or go with what is recommended by the framework creators.

Another option to is to go with a framework that lets you start small and make choices for your app as the need arises.

And you can do that with Vue.js.

Vue.js is called a *progressive framework* by its creators. This is because it allows you to start building your app with minimal effort as the core Vue.js library focuses only on the view layer. Over time as the requirements grow, you can adapt additional libraries for functionality.

The idea of adding features to the app you are creating over time doesn't limit the use of more complex development tools. Need to add a router? No problem; use the Vue-Router, a third-party option, or roll your own (see Chapter 11). Looking to manage in memory state? You can use a Plain Old JavaScript Object, a store pattern, or the Vue.js specific Vuex (see Chapter 6). By now you get the idea.

1

© Brett Nelson 2018
B. Nelson, *Getting to Know Vue.js*, https://doi.org/10.1007/978-1-4842-3781-6_1

This all probably makes Vue.js sound complicated, but it's not.

In fact, one of the reasons that developers often say they choose Vue.js is because of how easy it is to get started[12]. With little overhead, a developer can get to work and produce results without the added complexity of other popular frameworks. And this ease of beginning doesn't limit the complexity of the app you can build, as Vue.js can scale in complexity with your project's requirements.

Our First Vue.js Instance

One of the best parts of using Vue.js is that it requires little overhead to get started. Add a `script` tag referencing the Content Delivery Network (CDN) for the library to your page and you are ready to get going!

Let's take a quick look at what it requires to get started.

We will start with a pretty empty HTML file, shown in Listing 1-1.

Listing 1-1. Empty HTML File

```
<html lang="en">
<head>
<title>Getting to Know Vue.js</title>
</head>
<body>

</body>
</html>
```

To take this empty HTML file to a working Vue.js app, we need to add three things:

- An HTML element where we "mount" our app

- A <script> reference to Vue.js on the CDN

- A <script> element in which we create our app

---

[1]State of Vue.js 2017 https://cdn2.hubspot.net/hubfs/1667658/State_of_vue/State%20of%20 Vue.js%20report%202017%20by%20Monterail.pdf?t=1509106564387&utm_campaign=Vue. js&utm_source=hs_automation&utm_medium=email&utm_content=57726309&_hsenc=p2ANqtz-9Kq2JTU9inAkO5FNwcxKL65dVn9IRCqZ9P9OUeA8nqbyVTc4mOTL-I4FoKetfBkihubdO1E1rs9zR8xzvR NiBSo3ltGQ&_hsmi=57726309

[2]Adding Vue.js to Your Technology Stack https://www.monterail.com/services/vuejs-development

We will start with a place to mount the app. We will use a `<div>` with an id of `app`. For the second one, we will use the development version of Vue.js at `https://cdn.jsdelivr.net/npm/vue/dist/vue.js`. The final one will be a JavaScript `<script>` element that we will use for all our JavaScript to get started.

We could add the Vue.js `<script>` reference before the mounting point, but it would block the rest of the page from loading, making it seem slower to the user. The `<script>` element that will contain our app needs to be after the mounting point so that the DOM is ready for the app to load.

All this adds up to the contents of the `<body>` element shown in Listing 1-2.

Listing 1-2. The Structure of Our HTML Page

```
<!-- Div to Mount App -->
<div id="app">

</div>


<!-- Reference to Vue.js library -->
<script src="https://cdn.jsdelivr.net/npm/vue/dist/vue.js"></script>

<!-- Script Element for our first App -->
<script>

</script>
```

I've included comments in Listing 1-2 so it's easier to identify the items we are talking about.

That's all the setup we need before we create our first app. The next step is to add some template syntax to our app's `<div>` to bind some data to it. For this first app, we will use what is commonly called *mustache* syntax. It consists of two curly braces surrounding the property name we want to inject the data from, such as in `{{ propertyName }}`. This will make our app's `<div>` look like Listing 1-3.

Listing 1-3. The HTML Template for Our App

```
<!-- Div to Mount App -->
<div id="app">
    {{ propertyName }}
</div>
```

Now we just need to create the app.

In the empty `<script>` element we created, we are going to add a new instance of Vue.js, called `new Vue()`. Calling `new` on Vue without passing in an options object will not get us off to a good start. Therefore, we should at least tell it where to mount the app and give it a little data.

To tell our instance of Vue.js where to mount the options object, we pass in a property called `el`. The value for this will be the CSS selector. In our case, that is `#app` since we gave our `<div>` an `id` of `app`.

Note   If you want to know more about the `el` property of the Vue options, see Chapter 2's section on Vue options.

To give it some data, we will use the `data` property of the options object. The `data` property will be an object that has a property of the same name as the property name we used in our template binding. This means that our property name will be the very original and thought-out `propertyName`. In this case, we will give it a string that we want to show on the page.

Our `<script>` that we set aside for our app should now look like Listing 1-4.

Listing 1-4. Our First Vue App!

```
var app = new Vue({
    el: '#app',
    data: {
        propertyName: 'Hello from Getting to Know Vue.js!'
    }
});
```

Now when we look at our page in a web browser, we should see something like Figure 1-1.

Hello from Getting to Know Vue.js!

Figure 1-1. *Our first Vue.js app in action*

Congratulations, you made your first Vue.js app!

We'll be taking a closer look at what we did and how to use it as the starting point later on.

Developer Tools

Before we get too far, I want to explain some tools that I mention later on.

Browser Dev Tools

Throughout the course of this book, we will periodically be using tools built into the web browsers, commonly referred to as *dev tools*. While they can give us insight into what is going on with our JavaScript application, we can get greater insight by using the Vue-DevTools.

The Vue-DevTools come in two flavors—browser extensions for Chrome and Firefox and a standalone Electron app.

Links to the most up-to-date versions can be found at `https://github.com/vuejs/vue-devtools`.

Browsersync

In Figure 1-1, the address that the browser was viewing was `http://localhost:3000/`. This means it was being served from a server at localhost port 3000. Since I didn't deploy the `index.html` to a remote server or build a custom app to view it, I was able to use Browsersync for hosting the files locally. Unless otherwise noted, I will continue to use Browsersync (`https://www.browsersync.io/`) for loading files during local development.

To install Browsersync, Node.js and NPM are required. The good news is that both are installed when you install Node.js. Node.js can be installed by following the directions at `https://nodejs.org/`.

Once Node.js is installed, Browsersync can be installed for use anywhere on your computer by typing the command in Listing 1-5 at the command prompt.

Listing 1-5. The Install Browsersync Command

```
npm install -g browser-sync
```

To use Browsersync after it is installed, navigate to the directory that you want to serve files from in your command prompt and enter the command shown in Listing 1-6.

Listing 1-6. Starting Browsersync to Watch File Changes

```
browser-sync -w
```

The `browser-sync` portion of the command starts Browsersync. The `-w` is a flag that causes it to watch for file changes and reload the browser when a change is detected. This means we have to press refresh just a little less frequently.

When you run `browser-sync -w` at the command prompt, it should look somewhat like Figure 1-2.

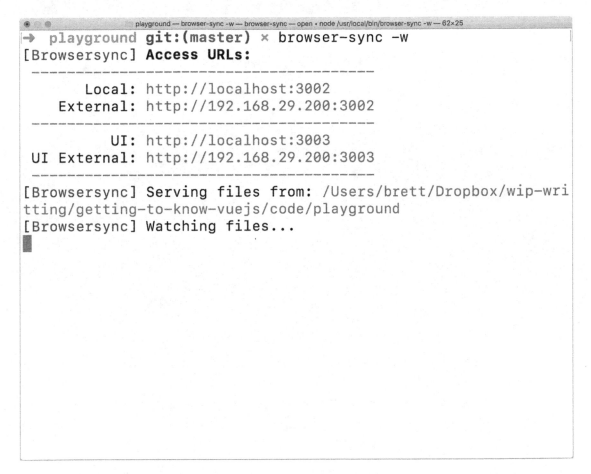

Figure 1-2. *Using Browsersync on the command line*

During this process, Browsersync should open your default browser to the address it shows for "local". With Figure 1-2 that means Firefox opened to `http://localhost:3002/` on my computer.

Summary

In this chapter, we looked at the value that Vue.js brings to developing a Single Page Application. We also built our first Vue app and looked at some tools that are useful when working with Vue.

CHAPTER 2

The Basics

Before we can get too far into understanding Vue, we need to cover a few things. We start off by learning what options we have when creating an instance of Vue. After we have an understanding of what we can provide Vue to make it suit our needs, we look at how we can start binding it to HTML, with a look at the templating syntax.

Vue Options

Before we get too far, we should learn more about the options that are available when creating a Vue instance. In Chapter 1, we created an instance by using the bare minimum of options to get Vue to render the `data` and the `el` property on the page in order to specify where the Vue instance should be and what data it would have access to.

Note   Technically, we could create a Vue instance with just the `el` property, but it couldn't do much.

El

The `el` property we talked about allows us to specify where our Vue instance will mount on the page. The value you provide can be a string that is a CSS selector (such as #app), as shown in Listing 2-1, or an HTMLElement, as shown in Listing 2-2.

Listing 2-1. Mounting Vue with a CSS Selector

```
var app = new Vue({
    el: '#app',
    data: {
```

© Brett Nelson 2018
B. Nelson, *Getting to Know Vue.js*, https://doi.org/10.1007/978-1-4842-3781-6_2

```
      propertyName: 'Hello from Getting to Know Vue.js! This was mounted
      by passing in an CSS Selector'
   }
});
```

Listing 2-2. Mounting Vue with an HTMLElement

```
var element = document.getElementById('app');
var app = new Vue({
   el: element,
   data: {
      propertyName: 'Hello from Getting to Know Vue.js! This was mounted
      by passing in an HTMLElement'
   }
});
```

When Vue is mounted to the HTML element that is provided, it replaces it with the Vue created DOM. The Vue DOM will contain the HTML that we provide as the template or the contents produced from the `render` function we provide. More on the `template` and `render` functions shortly.

If `template` and `render` are not provided, the HTML on the element that was provided as the mounting point will be used as the template for Vue to render the DOM. This is how we are able to inject our `propertyName` from the `data` into the HTML that was rendered without a template. It's not rendering the DOM created from our HTML, it's rendering the DOM created by Vue when it extracts the DOM we wrote and uses that as the template.

This is how Listing 2-3 becomes Figure 2-1.

Listing 2-3. No Template Vue App

```
<!-- Div to Mount App -->
   <div id="app">
      {{ propertyName }}
   </div>

   <!-- Reference to Vue.js library -->
   <script src="https://cdn.jsdelivr.net/npm/vue/dist/vue.js"></script>
```

```
<!-- Script Element for our App -->
<script>
    var app = new Vue({
        el: '#app',
        data: {
            propertyName: 'Hello from Getting to Know Vue.js!'
        }
    });
</script>
```

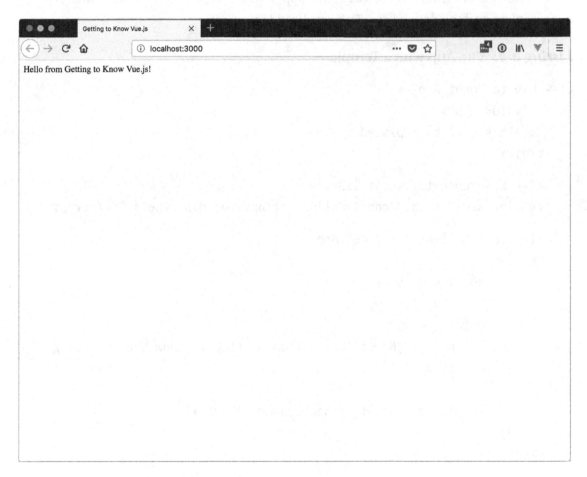

Figure 2-1. *Vue app rendered without a template*

Template

All this talk about Vue using a template means we should probably cover how to pass a template in as part of the options object. When you're creating a new Vue instance, one of the options you can provide as a property is `template`.

The `template` string is used by Vue to generate the DOM it will be placing in the web page in place of the element that was selected with the `el` option. It must have one root element. This will replace anything that is inside the element that the instance of Vue gets mounted to.

In Listing 2-4, the text inside `<div id="app">` will be replaced with the contents of our template and the data it uses. This results in Figure 2-2.

Listing 2-4. Vue App with a Template

```
<!-- Div to Mount App -->
    <div id="app">
        This will be replaced!
    </div>

    <!-- Reference to Vue.js library -->
    <script src="https://cdn.jsdelivr.net/npm/vue/dist/vue.js"></script>

    <!-- Script Element for our App -->
    <script>
        var app = new Vue({
            el: '#app',
            data: {
                propertyName: 'Hello from Getting to Know Vue.js! Using a
                template!'
            },
            template: '<div>{{ propertyName }}</div>'
        });
    </script>
```

Figure 2-2. *Vue app rendered with a template*

It is also possible to use the template property to provide a CSS selector to target an HTML element that has an ID. We do this by starting the template string with a hash tag (#). This can be done with a <script> element if you give it a type of x-template and it will not render on the page until Vue uses it as the template.

Note   You could use the <template> element instead of the <script> element to target a template by ID, but you should verify browser compatibility with your target audience first.

One point to keep in mind is that the element you target to use as a template should be placed before your app is declared. Listing 2-5 will render like Figure 2-3.

Listing 2-5. Vue App from a Template Using a querySelector

```
<!-- Script Element for our Template -->
<script id="myTemplate" type="x-template">
    <div>
        From Script Element Template: {{ propertyName }}
    </div>
</script>

<!-- Script Element for our App -->
<script>
    var app = new Vue({
        el: '#app',
        data: {
            propertyName: 'Hello from Getting to Know Vue.js! Using a
            template!'
        },
        template: '#myTemplate'
    });
</script>
```

Figure 2-3. *Vue app rendered with a template using querySelector*

Render

Sometimes creating a component requires a more programmatic approach than can be achieved with HTML or a string template. The render function is a way to programmatically create templates in JavaScript. The render function takes priority over templates and HTML templates.

Since this applies more to components and less to generic Vue understanding, the render function is covered more in depth in Chapter 8, "Using Components".

Data

We use the data property to tell our instance what shape our data will resemble. In Listing 2-6, the data has one property named propertyName. If there is something we want to be able to bind to in our Vue instance, we need to include it in the data *before* we create our Vue instance.

Listing 2-6. Data Has One Property Named propertyName

```
data: {
        propertyName: 'Hello from Getting to Know Vue.js!'
    }
```

When a new instance of Vue is created, it adds all the properties of data to a reactive system. The Vue reactive system monitors the properties of the data object for changes and updates the view to "react" to those changes.

This means we cannot add new data to be monitored by Vue's reactive system after the application starts. If, at the time you create your Vue instance, you don't know what the values of your data properties will be, define them with the names and give them a value of an empty string—", null, or undefined. Don't use the empty object {}, as that will render the stringified JSON of the empty object.

Say your HTML looked like Listing 2-7, with three data properties emptyObject, emptyString and nullProperty, and with values of an empty object, empty string, and null assigned accordingly in the app. In that case, the HTML would render like Figure 2-4. Notice how the emptyObject has brackets.

Listing 2-7. HTML with emptyObject, emptyString, and nullProperty

```
<!-- Div to Mount App -->
<div id="app">
    <p>emptyObject: {{ emptyObject }}</p>
    <p>emptyString: {{ emptyString }}</p>
    <p>nullProperty: {{ nullProperty }}</p>
</div>

<!-- Reference to Vue.js library -->
<script src="https://cdn.jsdelivr.net/npm/vue/dist/vue.js"></script>
```

```
<!-- Script Element for our App -->
<script>
    var app = new Vue({
        el: '#app',
        data: {
            emptyObject: {},
            emptyString: ",
            nullProperty: null
        }
    });
</script>
```

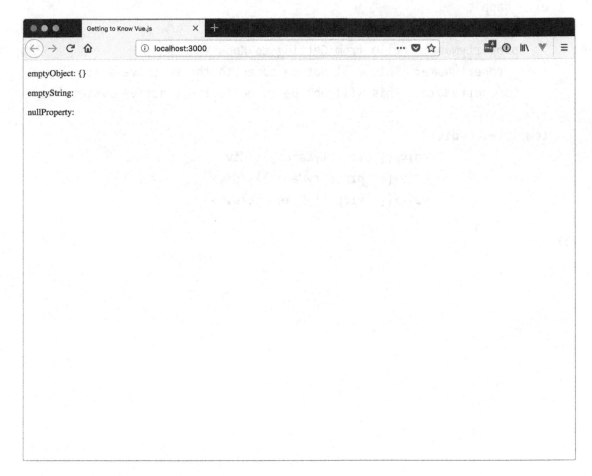

Figure 2-4. *Rendering empty values*

Names of the properties of the data object must not start with $ or _. Any properties that start with $ or _ will not be added to the reactive system, as they might cause conflicts with Vue's internal properties and methods. Since they won't be added to the reactive system, they also can't be accessed in the template.

Using a value that begins with either $ or _ in the template will cause an error. Listing 2-8 shows one property that starts with $ and one that starts with _. Trying to use these values in the template causes a reference error at runtime (see Figure 2-5), since Vue does not have references to these properties in the reactive system.

Listing 2-8. Trying to Use Data Properties That Start with $ or _

```
var app = new Vue({
    el: '#app',
    data: {
        propertyName: 'Hello from Getting to Know Vue.js!',
        _propertyName: 'This will not be added to the reactive system.',
        $propertyName: 'This will not be added to the reactive system.'
    },
    template: `<div>
                    <div>{{ propertyName }}</div>
                    <div>{{ _propertyName }}</div>
                    <div>{{ $propertyName }}</div>
                </div>`
});
```

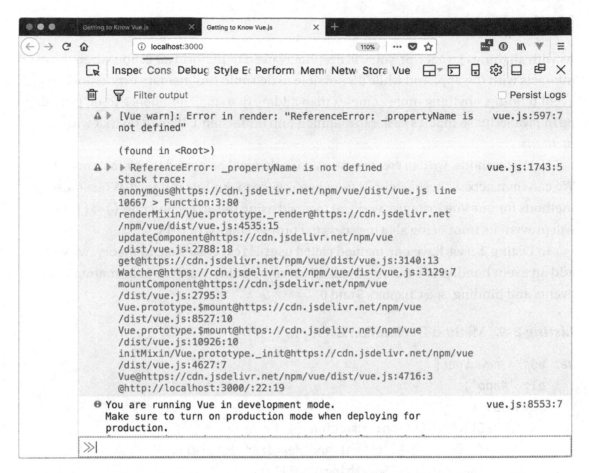

Figure 2-5. *Reference error, as Vue cannot find data properties that start with $ or _*

If you do include a property that starts with a $ or _, you can access it on your instance of Vue from the $data property.

When an instance of Vue is created, the data object originally included is added to the instance as a property with the name $data. So, if you assign your Vue instance to a variable called app, you can access the original data object at app.$data.propertyName. You will also be able to access it in methods using the this context instead of through a saved reference to the this.$data.propertyName instance.

Methods

As with all things JavaScript, you will eventually need to perform an action when the user interacts with the app. And while it's possible to do some rudimentary expressions in an event binding, anything more complex than adding two small numbers should probably be in JavaScript so that it's easier to maintain and understand. We can do that with *methods*.

Using methods, we can create custom code that will be bound to our instance of Vue. We can then access these methods from a reference to our Vue instance. When creating methods for our Vue instance, we need to avoid using the arrow function ()=>{}, as it will prevent us from being able to access the proper context of this.

In Listing 2-9 we have one method called userClickedAButton. In theory, we will add an event handler to a button to call this at some point. For more information about events and binding, see Chapters 5 and 6.

Listing 2-9. Method Declaration Example

```
var app = new Vue({
    el: '#app',
    methods: {
        userClickedAButton: function () {
            // Do Something Cool and Meaningful here!!!
            console.log('Something Cool!');
        }
    }
});
```

With the method in Listing 2-9, you can bind to an action or event. With the method in Listing 2-10, you can bind a method in the HTML template.

Listing 2-10. Binding a Method in the HTML

```
var app = new Vue({
    el: '#app',
    data: {
        text: 'Getting to Know Vue.js'
    },
    template: `<div>{{ capitalizeText() }}</div>`,
```

```
    methods: {
        capitalizeText: function () {
            return this.text.toUpperCase();
        }
    }
});
```

Note   To call a method from inside a method, we can use `this` to reference it, similar to how we reference the `data` property of `text` in Listing 2-10.

Listing 2-10 lets you perform a text transformation and displays properly. Figure 2-6 shows the working results.

Figure 2-6. *Binding HTML to a method*

Binding to a method isn't the preferred way to perform transformations like these. If you want to calculate a value to display the data you have access to in Vue, a computed property is more appropriate.

Computed Properties

Computed properties look very similar to methods, with one major difference—the results are cached. The values are updated only when the values that the computed property is based on change. In Listing 2-10, every time the page is rendered, the method is called to get the value. The computed property in Listing 2-11 achieves the same results as when we used a method, but it doesn't calculate the string on every render.

Listing 2-11. Computed Property

```
var app = new Vue({
    el: '#app',
    data: {
        text: 'Getting to Know Vue.js'
    },
    template: `<div>{{ capitalizedText }}</div>`,
    computed: {
        capitalizedText: function () {
            return this.text.toUpperCase();
        }
    }
});
```

Template Binding

The basic template syntax for Vue is pretty straightforward. We use *mustache* syntax to bind a property inside of HTML. Mustache syntax is the use of two curly braces surrounding your property, such as {{propertyName}}.

In the binding, you can also execute a JavaScript expression. This means that you can do some math, compare a property value, and display results based on the evaluation with the ternary expression, do some math, compare the results, and display some text depending on the results, or apply a method to the object you are binding. Listing 2-12 shows a few examples of adding numbers, performing comparisons, and displaying results, then changing a string to uppercase. The results of this app can be seen in Figure 2-7.

Listing 2-12. JavaScript Expressions in Bindings

```
var app = new Vue({
    el: '#app',
    data: {
        yes: 'Yes it is!',
        no: 'No it is not!',
        falseValue: false
    },
    template: `
        <div>
            <div>{{ 1 + 1 }}</div>
            <div>{{ falseValue === false ? yes : no }}</div>
            <div>{{ 1 == 2 ? yes : no }}</div>
            <div>{{ 1 + 1 + 1 > 2 ? yes : no }}</div>
            <div>{{ 'Getting to Know Vue.js'.toUpperCase() }}</div>
        </div>
        `

});
```

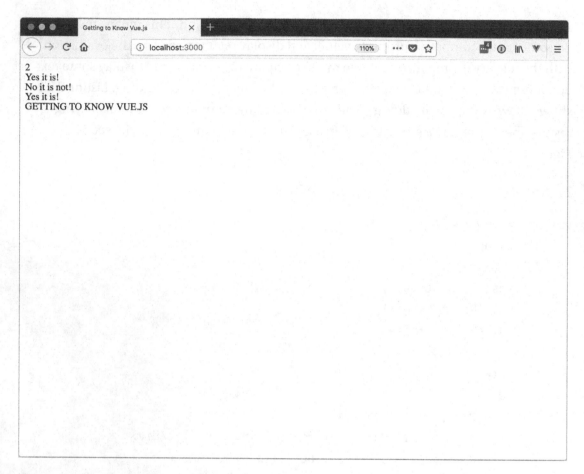

Figure 2-7. JavaScript expressions results

The mustache syntax works great for binding properties that are meant to be text, but it cannot be used to bind values to HTML element attributes. To bind to attributes, we will learn about our first Vue directive: v-bind.

To use the v-bind directive, you prepend it to the element's attribute that you want to bind to a value. In the place of the text you would normally be assigning, you provide the name of the property from your Vue instance.

In Listing 2-13, we use v-bind to assign a property to the name of the element. When we inspect the resulting page in Figure 2-8, we can see the name in the HTML

Listing 2-13. Dynamically Assigning a Name to a <div>

```
var app = new Vue({
    el: '#app',
    data: {
        myName: 'Cool Name'
    },
    template: `
        <div>
            <div v-bind:name="myName"></div>
        </div>
    `
});
```

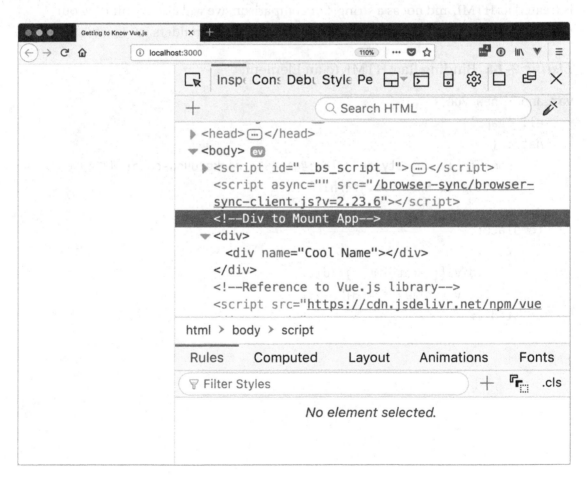

Figure 2-8. *Using v-bind to dynamically bind a value to the name of a <div>*

Another directive that we can use to bind data to the template is v-html. With v-html, the contents of the element that it is applied are replaced with the assigned value and are treated as HTML. This can be used when your requirements call for adding HTML that comes from a source outside your Vue app.

Caution   Only render HTML that you and your organization trust on your website. Never render HTML that users provide. Using untrusted HTML can lead to cross-site script vulnerabilities.

In Listing 2-14, we have a data property named someHTML that is a string of an <h1> element, which contains styles for the color and background-color of the element. Since we want this to render in our app, we bind it with the v-html directive so that it is treated as HTML and not as a string. For comparison, we will also try binding our someHTML with the mustache syntax, so we can see how that renders in Figure 2-9.

Listing 2-14. Binding Raw HTML to an Element

```
var app = new Vue({
    el: '#app',
    data: {
        someHTML: '<h1 style="color:#41b883; background-color:#35495e;">
        Getting to Know Vue.js</h1>'
    },
    template: `
        <div>
            <div>{{ someHTML }}</div>
            <div v-html="someHTML"></div>
        </div>
        `

});
```

Figure 2-9. *Binding raw HTML from a property to an element*

As we can see, the braces-bound someHTML was treated as a string.

Summary

In this chapter, we covered some aspects of the Vue instance, including how the reactive data system works, what the template is, and how Vue finds where it will be mounted in the web page. We also covered the template syntax that is used with Vue.

CHAPTER 3

Conditional Rendering

Sometimes your app will need to be able to determine whether or not to show something depending on user interactions. For instance, if we are creating a form that asks if users own a car and the user says no, there is no reason to show them the question that asks what color the car is.

Vue provides two directives to conditionally show content: `v-if` and `v-show`.

- With `v-show`, we can hide and show content using the CSS `display` property.

- With `v-if`, the content is removed from the DOM. It can be used with the `v-else` and `v-else-if` directives.

From a performance perspective, `v-show` has a higher initial render cost since it is rendered to the DOM even if the conditions to show it are `false`. `v-if` will not be rendered if the value is `false`. `v-show` does have less of a render cost when the value changes since it's already in the DOM and the CSS `display` property is the only change. On the other hand, `v-if` has to be added to the DOM when the condition to render it changes from `false` to `true`.

When you are trying to decide on using `v-if` or `v-show`, consider your use case. If the directive is going to change often, use `v-show`. If it is intended to change only occasionally or never after the first render, it's better to use `v-if`.

Now let's see how they work.

v-show

Using `v-show` is similar to using an HTML element attribute. The main difference is that the value you assign is from your Vue instance or an expression that evaluates to `true` or `false`. The expression can compare values from your Vue instance against values you set in the assignment or to other values in your Vue instance.

29

© Brett Nelson 2018
B. Nelson, *Getting to Know Vue.js*, https://doi.org/10.1007/978-1-4842-3781-6_3

When setting values for comparison, remember that the value you are assigning to v-show or v-if are not strings; they will be evaluated as JavaScript. v-show="show" is looking for the value of show in your Vue instance, not for the string "show". To use a string value in the expression, use single quotes ('my String') around it.

Listing 3-1 shows a few different examples of using v-show that can be seen in Figure 3-1:

1. Using true values from our Vue instance without comparison to show the content.

2. Using false values from our Vue instance without comparison to hide the content.

3. Comparing the value from our Vue instance with a string to show the content.

4. Comparing the value from our Vue instance with a string to hide the content.

5. Comparing a value from our Vue instance with a second value from our Vue instance to show the content.

6. Comparing the results of a little math to show the content.

7. Comparing the results of a little math to hide the content.

Listing 3-1. Using v-show to Show and Hide Elements Based on Expression Evaluations

```
var app = new Vue({
  el: '#app',
  data: {
    yes: true,
    no: false,
    maybe: 0,
    show: 'yes',
    dontShow: 'no',
    yesWord: 'yes'
  },
```

```
  template: `
    <div>
        <h1>
            1: <span v-show="yes">Yes</span>
        </h1>
        <h1>
            2: <span v-show="no">No</span>
        </h1>
        <h1>
            3: <span v-show="show == 'yes'">Yes!</span>
        </h1>
        <h1>
            4: <span v-show="dontShow == 'yes'">No :(</span>
        </h1>
        <h1>
            5: <span v-show="show == yesWord">Yes!</span>
        </h1>
        <h1>
            6: <span v-show="0 == 1 - 1">Yes!</span>
        </h1>
        <h1>
            7: <span v-show="0 == 1 + 1">No :(</span>
        </h1>
    </div>
    `
});
```

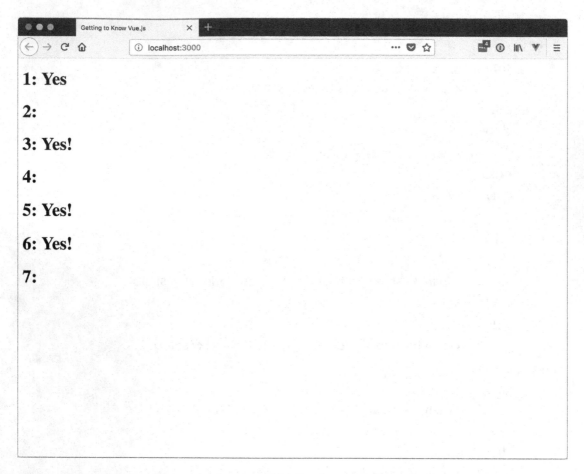

Figure 3-1. *Using v-show to show and hide elements based on expression evaluations*

With the way that v-show works, we can inspect the element and still see the content with its CSS display property set to none, as shown in Figure 3-2.

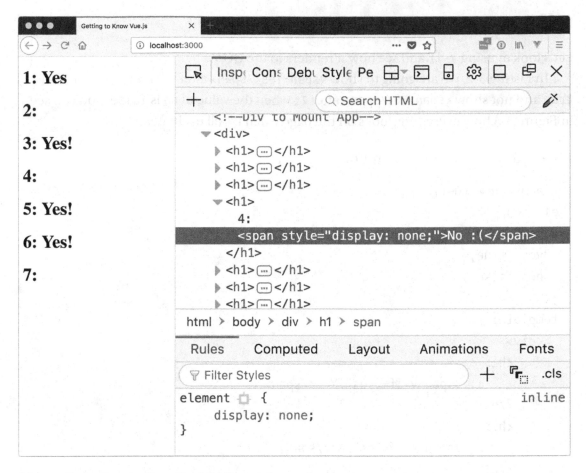

Figure 3-2. *Inspecting the hidden v-show element*

v-if v-else v-else-if

The other way to selectively render content is with v-if. Using v-if can range from the same use case as v-show, to the more complex with the use of v-else, to the most complex with v-else-if.

v-if

Let's look at using v-if and see how it renders to the DOM.

In Listing 3-2, we are going to show Yes after 1: if the value of yes is true and not show No after 2: when the value of no is false. You can see in Figure 3-3 how everything looks on the page when it's all evaluated.

Listing 3-2. Using v-if to Conditionally Render Elements

```
var app = new Vue({
  el: '#app',
  data: {
    yes: true,
    no: false
  },
  template: `
    <div>
        <h1>
            1: <span v-if="yes">Yes</span>
        </h1>
        <h1>
            2: <span v-if="no">No</span>
        </h1>
    </div>
    `
});
```

Figure 3-3. *The results of using v-if to conditionally render elements*

Since the contents of v-if are added to the DOM only if it evaluates to true, any false evaluations should not be visible in the inspector. Let's inspect the element that contains 2: and see if it is hiding a No (see Figure 3-4).

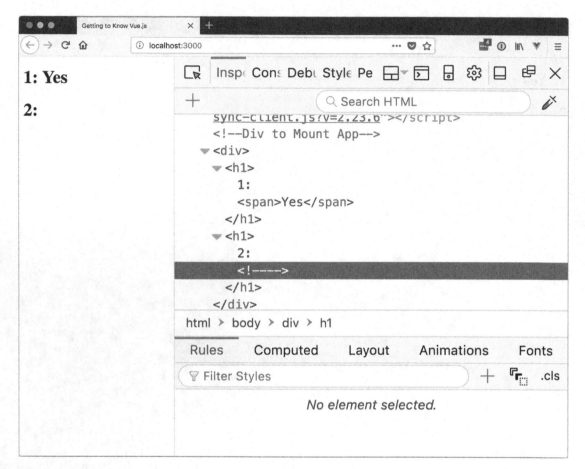

Figure 3-4. *Inspecting the contents to see where the "hidden" element is shows no content*

As we can see, `<span>No</span>` is not there.

v-else

Like all good if statements, `v-if` allows us to use an else, in this case `v-else`. With `v-else`, we can provide an option to display when `v-if` evaluates to `false`. `v-else` must follow a `v-if` or a `v-else-if` for it to work.

In Listing 3-3, we evaluate the value of no, which we set to `false`, and display the contents of the `v-else` in a `<h1>Show!</h1>` header. You can see the results in Figure 3-5. The inspected element shows that the `<h1>Don't Show</h1>` header is not present.

Listing 3-3. Using v-else to Conditionally Render Elements When v-if Evaluates to false

```
var app = new Vue({
  el: '#app',
  data: {
    no: false
  },
  template: `
    <div>
        <h1 v-if="no">Don't Show</h1>
        <h1 v-else>Show!</h1>
    </div>
    `
});
```

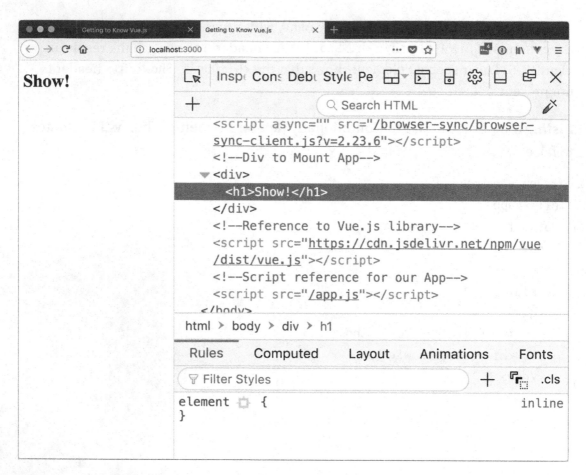

Figure 3-5. *Inspecting the use of v-else to conditionally render elements when v-if evaluates to false*

v-else-if

Sometimes you need to be able to selectively render one of many options. Perhaps in your app, for example, users must pick an account type and you have three or more account types. Or maybe you want to show results in a form based on a drop-down selection and there are more than three options in the drop-down menu. For that, we can use `v-else-if`. With `v-else-if`, we can chain `if` statements together, similar to using `if else` statements in JavaScript.

In our example, we have two sets of v-if—v-else-if and v-else—to look at. The first one shows the contents of the v-else-if element <h2>Else If</h2>. The second shows the contents of the v-else element <h2>Else</h2>. See Listing 3-4. You can see the results in Figure 3-6.

Listing 3-4. Using v-else-if

```
var app = new Vue({
  el: '#app',
  data: {
    yes: true,
    no: false
  },
  template: `
    <div>
      <div>
        <h1>Show v-else-if</h1>
        <h2 v-if="no">If</h2>
        <h2 v-else-if="yes">Else If</h2>
        <h2 v-else>Else</h2>
      </div>
      <div>
        <h1>Show v-else</h1>
        <h2 v-if="no">If</h2>
        <h2 v-else-if="no">Else If</h2>
        <h2 v-else>Else</h2>
      </div>
    </div>
    `
});
```

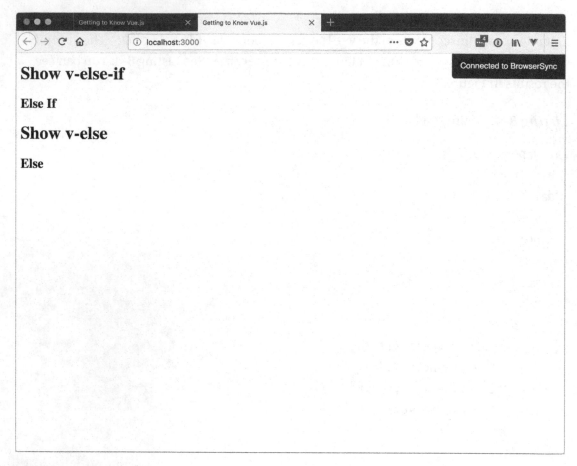

Figure 3-6. *Using v-else-if in action*

With the `v-if` group of directives, it is possible to group elements together so that you can show and hide them with one action instead of using `v-if` each time. To do this, wrap the elements to be shown and hidden in a `<template>` element. The `<template>` element will not be rendered if the `v-if` evaluates to `true`, but all the child elements will.

In Listing 3-5, we have two `<template>` elements—one to hide its contents and one to show it. The results can be seen in Figure 3-7.

Listing 3-5. Grouping v-if Elements

```
var app = new Vue({
  el: '#app',
  data: {
    yes: true,
    no: false
```

```
  },
  template: `
    <div>
      <template v-if="no">
        <h1>Don't show this</h1>
        <h2>It's a secret</h2>
      </template>
      <template v-if="yes">
        <h1>Show this</h1>
        <h2>We like to share</h2>
      </template>
    </div>
    `
});
```

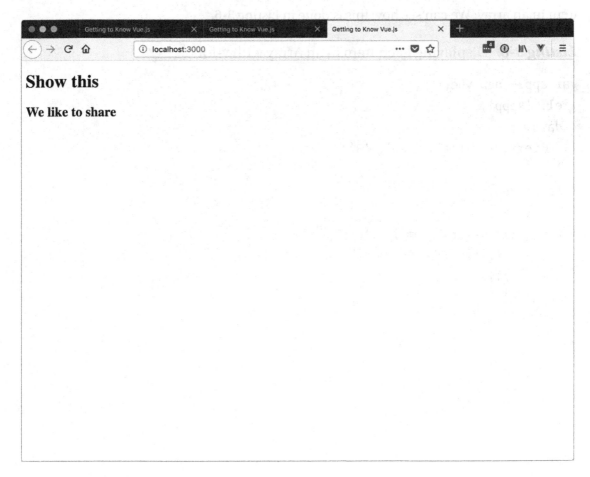

Figure 3-7. *Grouping v-if elements results*

Lists

Often developers must deal with groups of the same item, usually to display them on a web page. Although it can be *fun* to copy and paste the same snippet of code, Vue provides a directive to handle displaying array items, called v-for.

Tip   Don't actually copy and paste the same snippet of code; it's not fun.

Basics

With v-for, we can iterate (go over each item) through the items of an array and use each object to display content. In its simplest form, v-for can be used to display each item in an array. We can see how this is done in Listing 3-6.

Listing 3-6. Displaying Each Item in an Array with v-for

```
var app = new Vue({
  el: '#app',
  data: {
    items: ['first', 'two', '3']
  },
  template: `
    <ul>
      <li v-for="item in items">
        {{item}}
      </li>
    </ul>
  `
});
```

If you are familiar with the JavaScript for…in loop, this should look similar, as the v-for directive follows a similar setup. The item is the object that is used for each iteration and items is the collection that we are going through, or iterating through.

The element that v-for is placed on will be repeated for each item in the collection. In Listing 3-6, we make a new <li> and display the whole item. For this simple example, this is fine since each item is a string. For more complicated items, we need to use dot notation to display or use the properties of each item.

In case you are wondering, Listing 3-6 will display like Figure 3-8.

Figure 3-8. *v-for displaying an array of strings*

As the objects in your collection get more complicated, it is recommended that you use the :key attribute. The :key attribute is used by Vue to track the identity of the elements that have been rendered and update the DOM correctly.

Listing 3-7 shows a collection of books and uses the ID of each book as the key.

Listing 3-7. Using the :key Attribute with v-for

```
var app = new Vue({
  el: '#app',
  data: {
    books: [
      {
        title: 'Entertaining Kids Book',
        price: 4.99,
        id: 0,
        genres: ['kids', 'fiction']
      },
      {
        title: 'Teen Drama',
        price: 5.99,
        id: 1,
        genres: ['teen', 'fiction']
      },
      {
        title: 'Boring Facts',
        price: 6.99,
        id: 2,
        genres: ['adult', 'non-fiction']
      },
      {
        title: 'Overly Complex Story',
        price: 7.99,
        id: 3,
        genres: ['adult', 'science fiction', 'fiction']
      },
```

```
      {
        title: 'Facts for Teens',
        price: 3.99,
        id: 4,
        genres: ['teen', 'non-fiction']
      }
    ]
  },
  template: `
    <ul>
      <li v-for="book in books" :key="book.id">
        {{ book }}
      </li>
    </ul>
    `
});
```

Since our template still binds the items directly, similar to Listing 3-6, we will see the JSON object output for each item in the books array (see Figure 3-9). However, we shouldn't see any differences caused by the addition of the :key attribute.

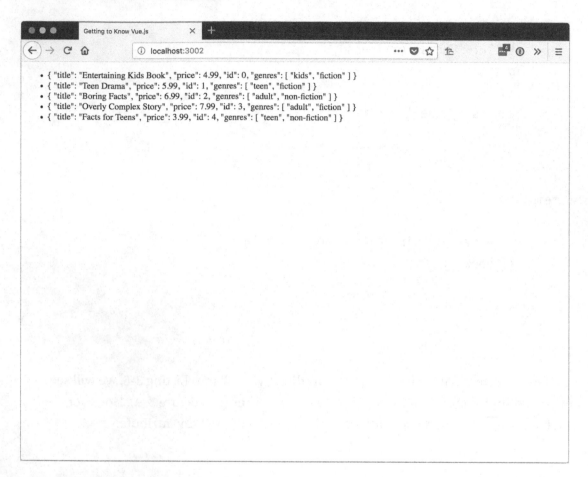

Figure 3-9. Using :key with v-for

Caution   It is possible to use `v-for` without using `:key`, but this should be done only if you are not going to alter the array index. If you are not using `:key`, you should avoid adding or removing items from the array except at the end or when sorting the array. Vue may not track and update all child elements that are repeated properly.

Accessing Object Properties

Let's clean up our display of books by rendering each value with some useful markup rather than dumping our JSON into an `<li>`.Listing 3-8 uses the same data that we used in Listing 3-7, so I will only show the template since that is where we are making changes.

Listing 3-8. Binding to Properties of an Item in v-for

```
template: `
  <ul>
    <li v-for="book in books" :key="book.id">
      <p><strong>Id:</strong> {{ book.id }}<p>
      <p><strong>Title:</strong> {{ book.title }}</p>
      <p><strong>Genres:</strong> <span v-for="genre in book.genres">
      {{genre}} </span></p>
    </li>
  </ul>
`
```

Here you can see that we are using dot notation to access the properties of each object. The more interesting part is that we also have a sub `v-for` for the genre of each book.

Note   Since `genres` is a simple object, I left off the `:`key attribute since we will not be using it to track the state of sub-components.

Looking at the results in Figure 3-10 makes me think we could help our genres list a little by adding some commas so it's easier to tell the genres apart.

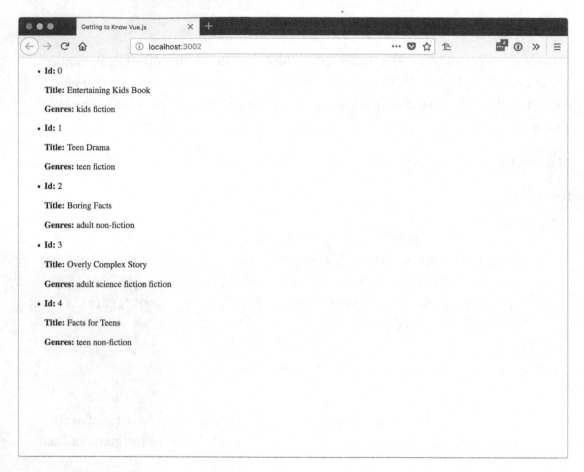

Figure 3-10. *Accessing object properties in v-for and using a v-for inside a v-for*

Index and Parent Properties

To conditionally render a comma after each genre, we will do a couple of things. We need to get the index of the current item. Thankfully, Vue provides us with the option to add a second parameter to v-for that gives us the index. To access this second parameter, we use parentheses to wrap our object and the index. So, v-for="book in books" becomes v-for="(book, index) in books" and we now know where we are in the array.

The other thing we need to know is the length of the array. We could count the items (five in this case) and use v-if to render a comma as long as the index is less than the length minus 1 (four in this case). This would work, but it's a simple example and sometimes (okay, most times) we will not know how long an array is going to be when we are writing the code. It's better to get the length of the array directly from the length parameter.

We can do this since we have access to all the properties of all the parent objects of our current row. In this case, from the v-for of the genres, we can access the books. genres array. Since we can access the array directly, we can use the length property of a JavaScript array to get the length.

This might be easier to see than read about. Listing 3-9 shows our updated use of v-for with the index property and the use of v-if to conditionally include a comma if the index is less than the length of the genres array minus 1.

Listing 3-9. Using v-for Index and Accessing Parent Properties

```
<span v-for="(genre, index) in book.genres">
  {{genre}}<span v-if="index < book.genres.length -1">, </span>
</span>
```

You can see that this cleans up the listing of genres so it's easier to read, as shown in Figure 3-11.

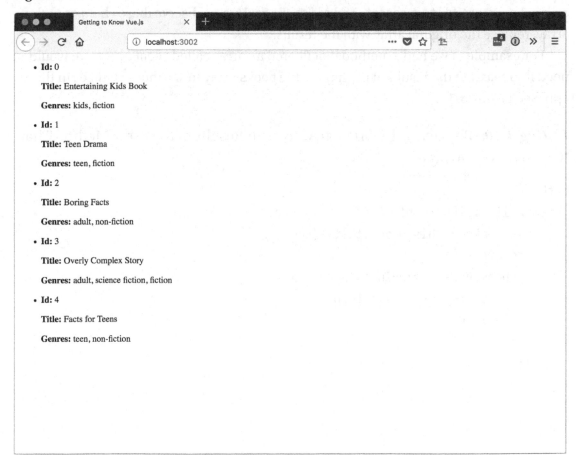

Figure 3-11. *Using index and parent properties in v-for*

Dealing with Change

Vue wraps observers around the following array mutation methods:

push
pop
shift
unshift
splice
sort
reverse

This means that as long as you are changing your array through these methods, Vue will be able to detect the changes. If you are using a method that does not mutate, or change, the original array, Vue will not detect that. The methods that do not change the original array are filter, concat, and slice. To get Vue to observe these changes to the array, replace the original array with the results.

For example, if we had a method that filtered an array called teenFilter, we would need it to reassign the results of the filter to the books array to see those changes in the app. See Listing 3-10.

Listing 3-10. Replacing the Original Array with Results of the Array Method That Returns a New Array

```
methods: {
  teenFilter: function() {
    this.books = this.books.filter(book => {
      return (
        book.genres.findIndex(genre => {
          return genre === 'teen';
        }) >= 0
      );
    });
  }
},
```

If you open the developer console in your web browser, you can call this method on your Vue instance with `app.teenFilter()` to see the results. They are shown in Figure 3-12.

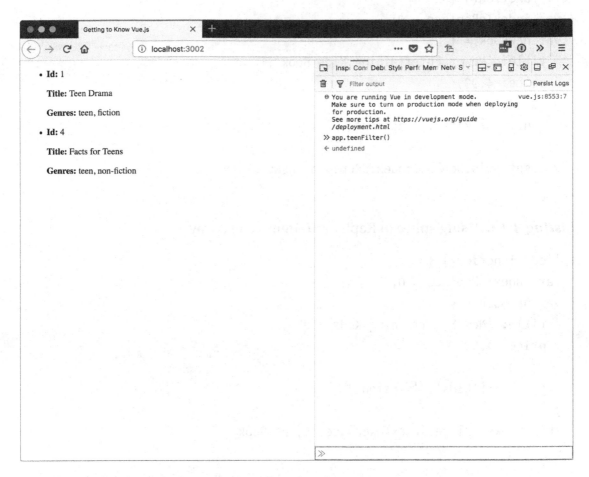

Figure 3-12. *Filtered array displayed with v-for*

When dealing with change and arrays, there are two cases that require special attention.

Vue cannot detect when an item is replaced in an array using the index of the item, and when the array is resized by assigning a new value to the `length` property. To get around these limitations, you can replace items in an array using `Vue.set`, like in Listing 3-11, or using the JavaScript `splice` method, like in Listing 3-12.

Listing 3-11. Using Vue.set to Replace an Item in an Array

```
set: function() {
  var indexToReplace = 0;
  var newBook = {
    title: 'Newer Entertaining Kids Book',
    price: 4.99,
    id: 0,
    genres: ['kids', 'fiction']
  };
  Vue.set(this.books, indexToReplace, newBook);
},
```

Listing 3-12. Using splice to Replace an Item in an Array

```
splice: function() {
  var indexToReplace = 0;
  var newBook = {
    title: 'New Entertaining Kids Book',
    price: 4.99,
    id: 0,
    genres: ['kids', 'fiction']
  };
  this.books.splice(indexToReplace, 1, newBook);
}
```

To resize an array, you can use the JavaScript splice method as well, as shown in Listing 3-13.

Listing 3-13. Using splice to Resize an Array

```
resize: function() {
  // Vue can not detect
  this.books.length = 1;
  // Use splice to resize an array, Vue can detect
  this.books.splice(0);
},
```

Objects

It is also possible to use v-for to go through the properties of an object. Since JavaScript engines behave differently, there is no guarantee about the order of the properties in different browsers.

The main difference in using v-for with an object instead of an array is that, with an object, when you use parentheses to access the value and the index, it accepts three parameters: value, key, and index. The value and index represent the same things as the array. The key represents the property name.

Listing 3-14 shows a single book object we will use to look at the properties. One of the properties is a function. In Figure 3-13, you can see that the function will be displayed in the HTML as it is written and not as the result of the method.

Listing 3-14. Using v-for with an Object

```
var app = new Vue({
  el: '#app',
  data: {
    book: {
      title: 'Overly Complex Story',
      price: 7.99,
      id: 3,
      genres: ['adult', 'science fiction', 'fiction'],
      action: function() {
        return 'I did an action';
      }
    }
  },
  template: `
    <ul>
      <li v-for="(prop, key, index) in book">
        {{index}}) {{key}}: {{prop}}
      </li>
    </ul>
    `
});
```

Figure 3-13. *Using v-for with an object*

If we want to display the results of the action function, we have to check for the type of each prop and invoke only the functions of our object. Listing 3-15 shows how we can use v-if with typeof on a <p> to achieve this; Figure 3-14 shows how it looks.

Listing 3-15. Checking Property Type in a v-for Loop

```
<p v-if="typeof prop == 'function'">{{prop()}}</p>
```

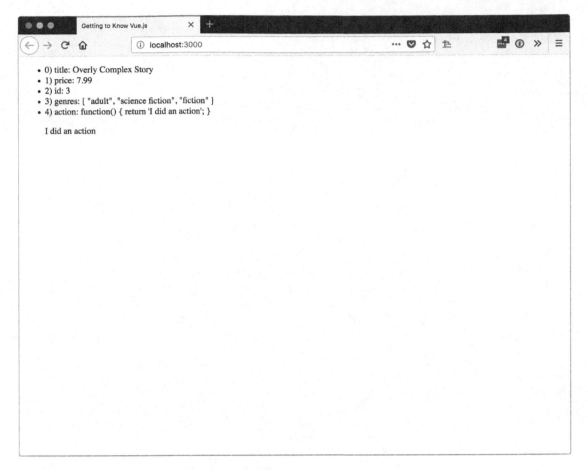

Figure 3-14. *Calling a function of the object in v-for*

We used `v-if` to invoke the function since `v-show` only hides the element with the CSS `display` property. If we used `v-show`, each `prop` would be invoked like it was a function and we would have a few unhandled errors.

Summary

In this chapter, we covered conditional rendering and the differences between `v-show` and `v-if`. We also covered rendering lists with the `v-for` directive and discussed how `v-for` can be used with arrays and objects.

CHAPTER 4

Computer Properties and Watchers

Using methods on your Vue instance to get formatted data is great, but it comes with the heavy toll of running every time the view is updated or re-rendered. We can avoid paying this performance toll by using computed properties. Sometimes we also need to be able to perform background, or asynchronous, tasks when the user interacts with the page, but we don't want to block the user from interacting. Vue provides us the option of using *watches* in these cases.

In this chapter, we will learn about computer properties and watchers and how to use them in Vue.

Computed Properties

Computed properties work similar to methods in Vue. The main difference is that the results are stored for later use, or cached, until one of the computed property's reactive dependencies change. The reactive dependencies were created by Vue when the instance was created with the new keyword. See Chapter 2, "The Basics," for more information about how Vue handles data changes.

To show the difference in behavior between methods and computed properties, Listing 4-1 uses four properties—three book titles formatted differently and a forth property of the publisher. These four properties will be combined to display the same text on the screen—"Getting to Know Vue.js by Apress".

In our template, we will display the text first by using the template syntax to format the message. Second, we will use a method to format the text, and last, we will use a computed property. The method and computed property both create a `console.log` when they are executed so we can see how often each runs.

57

© Brett Nelson 2018
B. Nelson, *Getting to Know Vue.js*, https://doi.org/10.1007/978-1-4842-3781-6_4

Listing 4-1. Comparing Template Syntax, Methods, and Computed Properties When Formatting Text

```
var app = new Vue({
  el: '#app',
  data: {
    bookNameForTemplate: 'Getting to Know Vue.js',
    bookNameForMethod: 'Getting to Know Vue.js',
    bookNameForComputed: 'Getting to Know Vue.js',
    publisher: 'Apress'
  },
  methods: {
    getTitleBlurb: function() {
      console.log('Called: getTitleBlurb');
      return `${this.bookNameForMethod} by ${this.publisher}`;
    }
  },
  computed: {
    titleBlurb: function() {
      console.log('Called: titleBlurb');
      return `${this.bookNameForComputed} by ${this.publisher}`;
    }
  },
  template: `
    <div>
        <h3>Template based:</h3>
        <h4>{{bookNameForTemplate}} by {{publisher}}</h4>

         <h3>Method based:</h3>
         <h4>{{getTitleBlurb()}}</h4>

         <h3>Computed Property based:</h3>
         <h4>{{titleBlurb}}</h4>

    `
});
```

In Figure 4-1, we can see that all three ways render the same result. Looking at the developer console reveals that the method `getTitleBlurb` and the computed property `titleBlurb` each ran once.

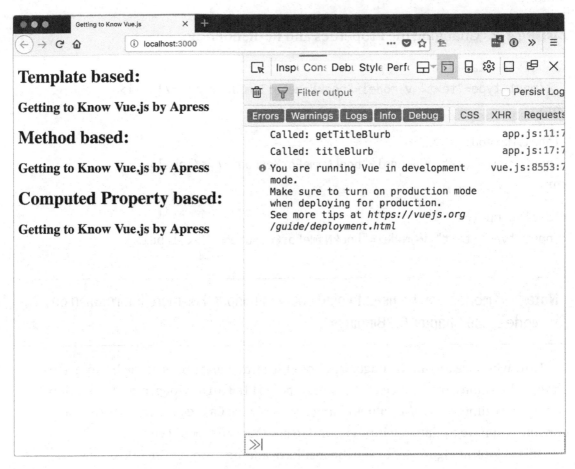

Figure 4-1. *Three ways to render the same result*

But what if the view had to re-render?

Let's add three `<input>`s and bind each one to a different bookName with `v-model`. The update to the template will add the lines in Listing 4-2 to our template near the bottom.

Listing 4-2. Changing the Properties and Re-Rendering

```
<label>Template:
  <input type="text" v-model="bookNameForTemplate" /></label>
<br>

<label>Method:
<input type="text" v-model="bookNameForMethod" /></label>
<br>

<label>Computed:
<input type="text" v-model="bookNameForComputed" /></label>
```

Note   `v-model` can be used to bind data to an input. For more information on `v-model`, see Chapter 6, "Bindings".

Now when we reload the page, we should see three text boxes at the bottom. If we change the values, we will see that `Called: getTitleBlurb` is logged to the developer console any time any of the values change. We only see `Called: titleBlurb` in the console when we update the input bound to `bookNameForComputed`.

Take a look at Figure 4-2 to see the results of adding " too" to the book titles.

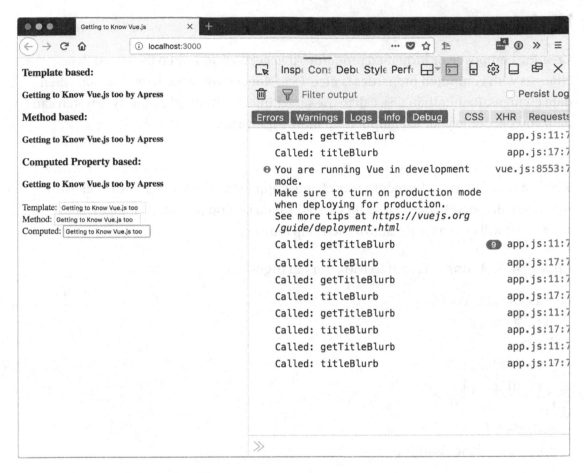

Figure 4-2. *Updating the data*

We can see that `Called: getTitleBlurb` was called 12 times, once for each character entered. `Called: titleBlurb` was logged four times since the computed property only changed when its dependent property was updated.

In our simple example, this don't seem like it would be that big of an issue, but what if you had to call the server for each of those changes? The difference would add up quickly.

How many times did formatting with the template get called? Every time.

Watchers

Creating composite or formatted properties that get updated when the based data changes with computed properties is nice. Occasionally you need to take action when data changes. Rather than tie a call to the server into a computed property, a watch can help you decouple your user input from more expensive tasks.

Listing 4-3 uses the Axios library, https://github.com/axios/axios, to call the Star Wars API, https://swapi.co/, to get a list of star ships when the user enters text into a search box. We won't be monitoring changes applied to the input, but we will use a watch to call the API and get a result when the data behind the input changes. For the results, we will display the name of each ship returned.

Listing 4-3. Using a Watch to Monitor Changes

```
var app = new Vue({
  el: '#app',
  data: {
    searchText: ",
    results: []
  },
  methods: {
    search: function() {
      axios
        .get(`https://swapi.co/api/starships/?search=${this.searchText}`)
        .then(response => {
          this.results = response.data;
        });
    }
  },
  watch: {
    searchText: function(newSearchText, oldSearchText) {
      this.search();
    }
  },
  template: `
    <div>
    <label>Search:
```

```
<input type="text" v-model="searchText" /></label>

<h5>Results: <small>{{results.count}}</small></h5>

<ul>
  <li v-for="result in results.results">
    {{result.name}}
  </li>
</ul>
</div>
`

});
```

If we run this and type in the search box, we will experience a slight delay and then results will start to display in a list. If we enter x, we should see something like Figure 4-3.

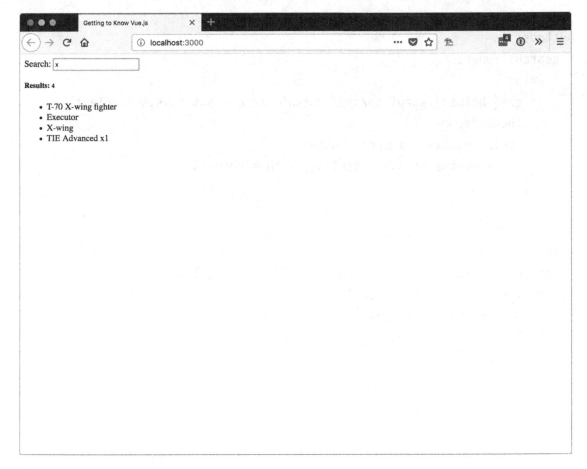

Figure 4-3. *Watch in action*

New and Old Values

When a watch is invoked, it is passed the new value and the old value. We didn't do anything with them at this time, but you could perform checks to verify that you want to take action on the new value.

For instance, we could not call the API if the new value was the same as a previous value. In Listing 4-4, we store the results in a `history` property so we can access the previous searches again without making a second call.

Listing 4-4. Using the New Value Provided When a Watch Is Called

```
data: {
  searchText: ",
  results: [],
  history: {}
},
methods: {
  search: function() {
    axios
      .get(`https://swapi.co/api/starships/?search=${this.searchText}`)
      .then(response => {
        this.results = response.data;
        this.history[this.searchText] = this.results;
      });
  }
},
watch: {
  searchText: function(newSearchText, oldSearchText) {
    if (this.history[newSearchText]) {
      this.results = this.history[newSearchText];
    } else {
      this.search();
    }
  }
},
```

As you can see, if the `newSearchText` is a property on our `history` object, we get the value we have stored; otherwise, we make the call to the API.

Deep

Some objects are more complex than a search string but still require a watch. We can use the deep property to watch the nested properties of an object. To set deep to true, we will set our watch to an object with two properties: handler is the function that gets called when the watch is triggered and deep is set to true so we can monitor changes in the object.

In Listing 4-5, we can see how a deep watch is set up. Any time a change happens to the book, the watch will call the handler and we will see Book Changed logged to the developer console, as shown in Figure 4-4.

Listing 4-5. Watching for Changes on Nested Properties

```
var app = new Vue({
  el: '#app',
  data: {
    book: {
      title: 'Getting to Know Vue.js',
      publisher: 'Apress',
      year: 2018
    }
  },
  watch: {
    book: {
      handler: function(newBook, oldBook) {
        console.log('Book Changed');
      },
      deep: true
    }
  },
  template: `
    <div>
    <label>Search:
    <input type="text" v-model="book.title" /></label>
    <ul>
      <li v-for="(value, prop) in book">
```

```
      {{prop}}: {{value}}
    </li>
  </ul>
  </div>
  `

});
```

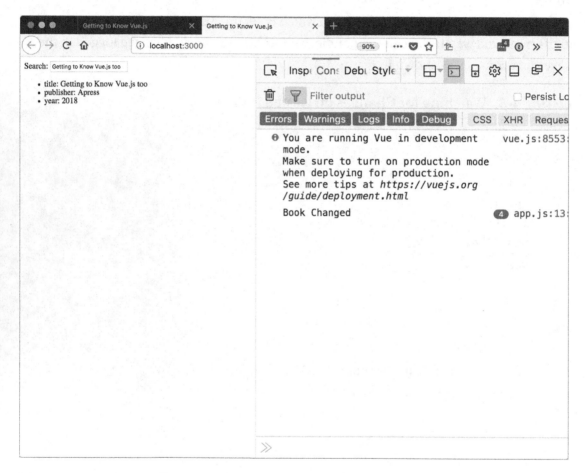

Figure 4-4. *Using a deep watch to monitor object property changes*

Immediate

The other option you can use with a watch is immediate. With immediate set to true, Vue will call the watch when your Vue instance loads with the current value. This way, you can be sure it fires at least once.

Listing 4-6 shows how to use the `immediate` property with a watch. Figure 4-5 shows its results.

Listing 4-6. Setting immediate to true on a Watch

```
watch: {
    book: {
        handler: function(newBook, oldBook) {
            console.log('Book Changed');
        },
        immediate: true
    }
},
```

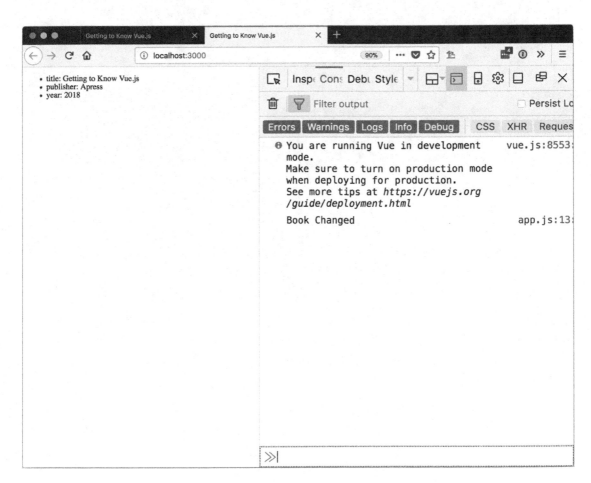

Figure 4-5. *The watch fires even if no change is made to the object*

Summary

In this chapter we covered computed properties and watchers. With computed properties, we can format responses and access them like data values, but they are cached so we don't have to recalculate them every time we use them. Watches provide us with a way to respond to values that change in an asynchronous manner.

CHAPTER 5

Events

Being able to display lists of items and reuse portions of our markup is great for displaying things, but sometimes we want the user to do something and that is where *events* come in. In this chapter, we will learn about using *listeners* to wait for events, *event handlers* to take action when an event is called, and *modifiers,* which we can apply to events.

Listeners

Setting up event listeners in Vue is pretty straightforward. On the element from which you want to listen to events, add an attribute of `v-on:eventName="handleEvent"`, where `eventName` is the name of the event you are interested in and `handleEvent` is how you want to handle the event.

So if we wanted to listen to the click event on an `<h1>` element that would change a value between `true` and `false`, we would add `v-on:click="value = !value"`. It would look something like Listing 5-1. In the browser, it would look like Figure 5-1 before we click anything and Figure 5-2 after we click the word "Toggle".

Listing 5-1. Using v-on To Listen To Click Events

```
var app = new Vue({
  el: '#app',
  data: {
    show: true
  },
  template: `
    <div>
        <h1 v-on:click="show = !show">
            Toggle
```

© Brett Nelson 2018
B. Nelson, *Getting to Know Vue.js*, https://doi.org/10.1007/978-1-4842-3781-6_5

```
        </h1>
        <p v-show="show">
            Hide and show this message by clicking the word "Toggle"
        </p>
    </div>
    `

});
```

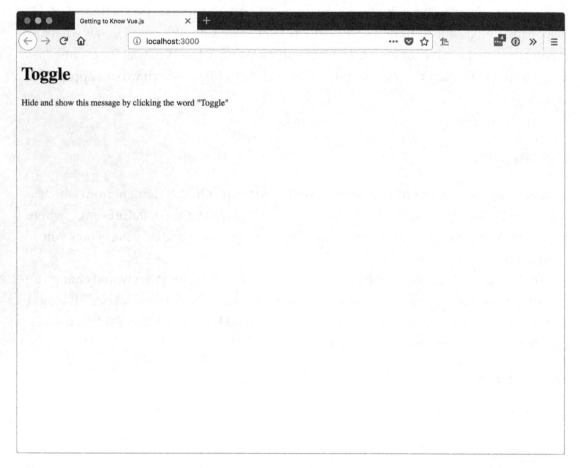

Figure 5-1. *Our v-on:click event before clicking Toggle*

Figure 5-2. *Our v-on:click event after clicking Toggle*

This is done to bind to any event, so with native HTML elements you can change the click to `dblclick` or `pointerenter` and still get the event to fire and show or hide the message.

Your question might be, "What else can I do when an event fires besides show a simple expression?". I'm glad you asked because that brings us to event handlers.

Handlers

Event handlers are used to handle events when they are raised. We use a handler method since trying to accomplish much more than a variable assignment in the expression would get cumbersome.

Methods

To move our logic for handling the click event from Listing 5-1 to a method, we need to create a method in our Vue instance. Let's call it toggle. In our toggle method, we will do the same thing we were doing with the expression handler—change the value of show between true and false. To use our new method, we use the name of toggle as the value that we assign to v-on:click. Listing 5-2 shows the complete toggling app.

Listing 5-2. Using a Method to Handle the Click Event

```
var app = new Vue({
  el: '#app',
  data: {
    show: true
  },
  methods: {
    toggle: function() {
      this.show = !this.show;
    }
  },
  template: `
    <div>
        <h1 v-on:click="toggle">
            Toggle
        </h1>
        <p v-show="show">
            Hide and show this message by clicking the word "Toggle"
        </p>
    </div>
    `
});
```

Inline Method

Perhaps you want to create a more versatile method by allowing it to take a parameter as opposed to inverting a Boolean value. That is possible as well. In Listing 5-3, we have two <h1> elements: one that displays Show and uses an inline handler to call setShow with the value of true, and one that displays Hide and uses an inline handler to call setShow with the value of false. With a new method that accepts a value and assigns it to show, we can show or hide the message. We cannot toggle in the same manner, by clicking the same word repeatedly, since hide always sets show to false and show always sets show to true.

Listing 5-3. Using Inline Handlers to Pass a Value to a Method

```
var app = new Vue({
  el: '#app',
  data: {
    show: true
  },
  methods: {
    setShow: function(newValue) {
      this.show = newValue;
    }
  },
  template: `
    <div>
    <h1 v-on:click="setShow(true)">
        Show
    </h1>
    <h1 v-on:click="setShow(false)">
        Hide
    </h1>
        <p v-show="show">
            Hide and show this message by clicking "Hide" or "Show"
        </p>
    </div>
    `
});
```

One added thing you can do with an inline handler is pass the DOM event into the method using the $event variable. In the method handler, you can then access properties and methods of the event. In Listing 5-4, we pass the event to our handler and log the type to the developer console. You can see in Figure 5-3 that clicking on the Show and Hide <h1>s causes click events in the developer console.

Listing 5-4. Passing DOM Event with Inline Event Handler

```
var app = new Vue({
  el: '#app',
  data: {
    show: true
  },
  methods: {
    setShow: function(newValue, event) {
      if (event) {
        console.log(event.type);
      }
      this.show = newValue;
    }
  },
  template: `
    <div>
    <h1 v-on:click="setShow(true, $event)">
        Show
    </h1>
    <h1 v-on:click="setShow(false, $event)">
        Hide
    </h1>
        <p v-show="show">
            Hide and show this message by clicking "Hide" or "Show"
        </p>
    </div>
    `
});
```

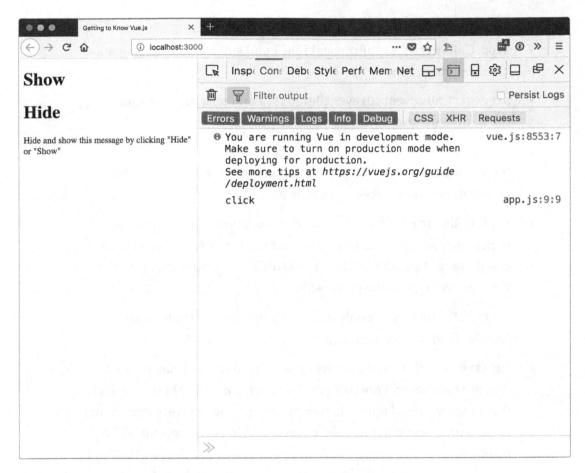

Figure 5-3. *Logging the event type to the developer console*

Modifiers

Event modifiers allow us to declaratively change an event's behavior. *Declaratively* means when we want to modify the behavior of an event, we declare it in the markup. We are not assigning the modification from somewhere in the JavaScript. This allows us to see the modifications where we register the event handlers in the markup and leave the handler methods to be just the parts of code needed to handle the event.

To apply a modifier, we use dot notation on the event name. If we were binding to a click event and wanted to add the capture modifier, our v-on would look something like v-on:click.capture="methodName".

Some of the event modifiers that Vue provides are:

- `stop`: Calls `event.stopPropagation()` and stops further propagation of the current event.

- `prevent`: Calls `event.preventDefault()` and tells the user agent to not handle the event with its default handler.

- `capture`: Adds the event listener in capture mode. Using capture mode for the event will allow our handler to be called before the target of the event will get to handle it.

- `self`: Calls the handler only if the event starts on the element we register the handler on. This saves us the extra work of checking the `event.target` to limit our handler to only events that start on the element we register the event with.

- `once`: Calls the handler only once without us having to remove the handler from the element when we handle the event.

- `passive`: Sets the event handler option of passive to `true`, meaning that the handler will not call `event.preventDefault()` and if it does, the browser should ignore it. Passive event handlers were introduced to help browsers provide a more consistent look with events while scrolling.

Using a Modifier

Let's look at how this works, but before we do, let's see how a click event propagates through some `<div>`s. We will have four `<div>`s: two inner `<div>`s with "Inner One" and "Inner B" text will be inside a `<div>` that has "Middle" text, and a fourth `<div>` with the text "Outer". Each `<div>` will have a click handler that pushes the `<div>`'s text onto an array of `messages`.

We will display the messages with `v-for` after our collection of `<div>`s and add a button to clear the messages at the bottom of the page. Looking at Listing 5-5 will give you a better understanding.

Listing 5-5. Event Propagations Setup

```
var app = new Vue({
  el: '#app',
  data: {
    messages: []
  },
  template: `
    <div>
        <div v-on:click="messages.push('Outer')">
            <h4>Outer</h4>

            <div v-on:click="messages.push('Middle')">
                <h4>Middle</h4>

                <div v-on:click="messages.push('Inner One')">
                    <h4>Inner One</h4>
                </div>

                <div v-on:click="messages.push('Inner B')">
                    <h4>Inner B</h4>
                </div>
            </div>
        </div>
        <p>
            Last clicked:
            <ol>
                <li v-for="message in messages">
                    {{message}}
                </li>
            </ol>
            </p>
        <input type="button" v-on:click="messages = []" value="Clear" />
    </div>
    `

});
```

This will look like Figure 5-4 in the browser.

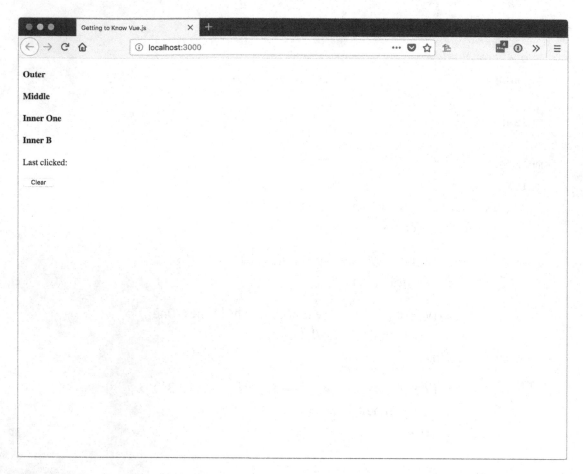

Figure 5-4. *Event propagations setup in the browser*

This isn't too exciting yet, but let's take a look at the order in which the events are called. Figure 5-5 shows what happens when we click on the words "Inner B".

Figure 5-5. *Click event handled as it travels up the DOM tree*

Clicking on "Inner B" causes the event to be handled by "Inner B", "Middle", and then "Outer". If we click on "Middle", we will see only "Middle" and "Outer".

If we wanted to stop propagation when "Inner One" is clicked and not have the other events fire, we would use the stop modifier. You can see how to apply the stop modifier in Listing 5-6.

Listing 5-6. Using the Stop Modifier

```
<div v-on:click.stop="messages.push('Inner One')">
    <h4>Inner One</h4>
</div>
```

Now when we click on "Inner One", only "Inner One" will be added to our messages array for display. Figure 5-6 shows the results.

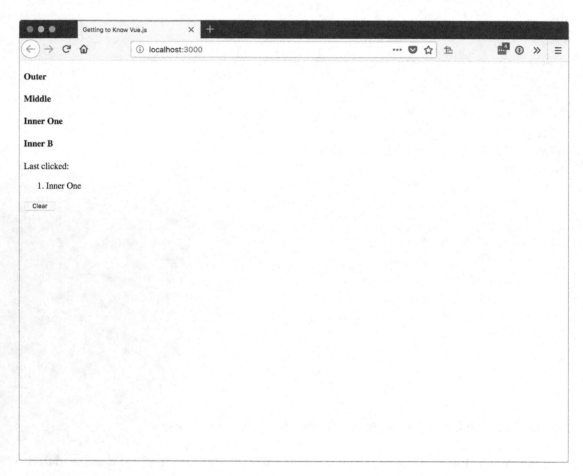

Figure 5-6. *Using the stop modifier to prevent event propagation*

Chain Modifiers

It is also possible to chain modifiers. If we add `capture` and `once` to our middle <div> and click on "Inner B" twice, we will see "Middle" happen first on the first click but not happen on the second click. Listing 5-7 shows the code, and Figure 5-7 shows the results.

Listing 5-7. Chaining Modifiers

```
<div v-on:click.once.capture="messages.push('Middle')">
```

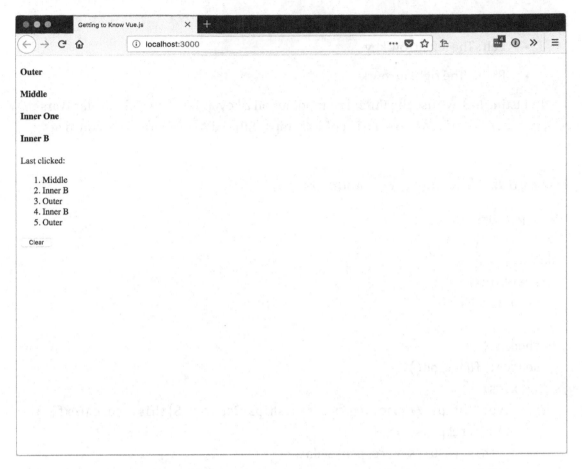

Figure 5-7. *Clicking twice on Inner B without chain modifiers on Middle*

Input

There are modifiers for inputs as well by adding one of the following to a key event:

- Enter: The Enter or Return key

- Tab: The Tab key

- Delete: The delete or backspace key

- Esc: The Escape key

- Space: The spacebar

- Up: The up arrow key

- Down: The down arrow key

- Left: The left arrow key

- Right: The right arrow key

In Listing 5-8, we use the Enter key modifier on a keyup event to call the Star Wars API, `https://swapi.co/`, to get a list of star ships with the Axios library, as shown at `https://github.com/axios/axios`.

Listing 5-8. Using Key Event Modifiers

```
var app = new Vue({
  el: '#app',
  data: {
    searchText: ",
    results: []
  },
  methods: {
    search: function() {
      axios
        .get(`https://swapi.co/api/starships/?search=${this.searchText}`)
        .then(response => {
          this.results = response.data;
        });
    }
  },
  template: `
      <div>
      <label>Search:
        <input
            type="text"
            v-model="searchText"
            v-on:keyup.enter.esc="search" />
      </label>

      <h5>Results: <small>{{results.count}}</small></h5>
```

```
<ul>
  <li v-for="result in results.results">
    {{result.name}}
  </li>
</ul>
</div>
`

});
```

Now when we want to perform a search, we need to press Enter when we are in the searchText input. In Figure 5-8, you can see that we make only one call to the API for the search.

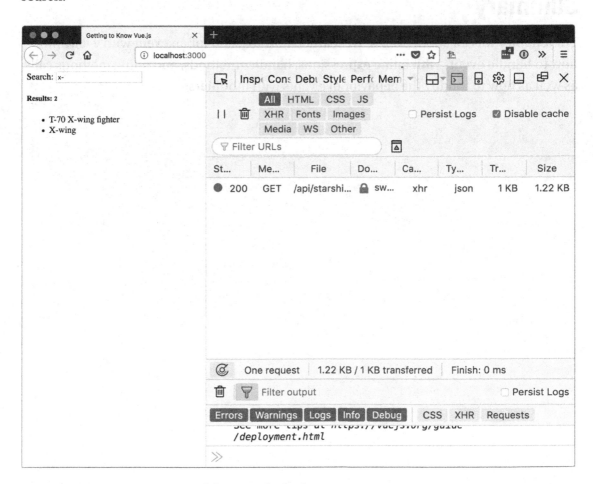

Figure 5-8. *Using Key modifiers with the keyup event*

Key event modifiers can be chained as well. In Listing 5-9 you can see how to add the Escape key modifier, so search can be triggered with either the Enter key or the Escape key.

Listing 5-9. Chaining Input Event Modifiers

```
<input
    type="text"
    v-model="searchText"
    v-on:keyup.enter.esc="search" />
```

Summary

This chapter was all about events! We learned how to listen for an event with `v-on` and how to handle events with inline expressions, handler methods, and inline methods calls as well as how to modify the behavior of e vents with modifiers

CHAPTER 6

Bindings

One of the main reasons to use a framework like Vue is that it makes responding to user input easier. One of the places user input is common is in forms. We also like to update the look of this when users make an input/select an option, changing styles and classes to let the user know something happened.

In this chapter, we will learn about binding data to form input along with binding to inline styles and classes.

Forms

Getting user input out of a form and into a variable we can manage is one of the main advantages of using a framework like Vue. Vue provides us with the v-model directive to bind data to our inputs.

v-model

With v-model, we will have two-way data binding from the backing data variable to the UI. With two-way data binding if the user makes a change to the data model via a method, we will see the UI display the update. If we make a change in the UI, the data model will be updated.

An important thing to understand is that Vue will not use the value or checked or selected attributes of the elements. The data model created when the Vue instance is initialized is the ultimate source of truth for Vue.

Note   The backing data is the data stored in the Vue instance data property.

© Brett Nelson 2018
B. Nelson, *Getting to Know Vue.js*, https://doi.org/10.1007/978-1-4842-3781-6_6

Inputs

For the following `<input/>` examples, the data model will look like Listing 6-1 with inputs that contain a property for each example ahead.

Listing 6-1. The Input Example Data Model

```
data: {
  inputs: {
    text: '',
    numberAsString: 0,
    numberAsNumber: 0,
    date: '',
    password: '',
    checkbox: false,
    checkboxes: [],
    radios: '',
    radiosPreset: 'rollout',
    radiosDynamic: '',
    radiosDynamicOptions: [
      {
        label: 'Blue',
        value: 'Light'
      },
      {
        label: 'Red',
        value: 'Dark'
      }
    ],
    file: '',
    select: '',
    multiselect: []
  },
```

Each example will also have an output, so we can see what the model contains as we interact with the `<input/>`.

Text

Almost all forms are going to need a text input of some sort. To bind our data to the text input, we add `v-model="inputs.text"` as an attribute. Our input should look like Listing 6-2 with its accompanying model display. You can see how this looks in the browser in Figure 6-1.

Listing 6-2. Text Input Data Binding

```
<h4>Text</h4>
<input type="text" v-model="inputs.text" />
<p>
    <strong>Text:</strong> {{inputs.text}}
</p>
```

Figure 6-1. *Text input data binding in the browser*

87

Number

Number `<input/>` binds the same way as text with `v-model="inputs.numberAsString"`. It also doesn't convert the value of our input to a number, so the data model will contain a string. We can convert the number in a method or we can use the `.number` modifier. To bind with the modifier, we add the following as an attribute `v-model.number="inputs. numberAsNumber"`. To see the type of number contained in the data model, we add an output that shows the `typeof` the value we are looking at.

Listing 6-3 shows two inputs with two outputs each. The outputs are the value and the `typeof` for the value of each input. You can see in Figure 6-2 when we enter 4 into both inputs that the type of `numberAsString` is string and the type of `numberAsNumber` is number.

Listing 6-3. Binding to Number Inputs with Types Displayed

```
<h4>Number as String</h4>
<input type="number" v-model="inputs.numberAsString" />
<p>
    <strong>Number:</strong> {{inputs.numberAsString}}
</p>
<p>
    <strong>Typeof numberAsString:</strong> {{typeof inputs.
    numberAsString}}
</p>

<h4>Number as Number</h4>
<input type="number" v-model.number="inputs.numberAsNumber" />
<p>
    <strong>Number:</strong> {{inputs.numberAsNumber}}
</p>
<p>
    <strong>Typeof numberAsNumber:</strong> {{typeof inputs.
    numberAsNumber}}
</p>
```

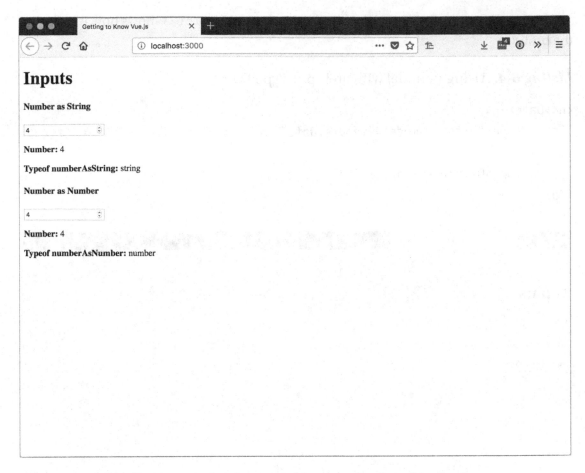

Figure 6-2. Binding to number inputs with types displayed in the browser

Date

The Date `<input/>`s look a little different in each browser, but the results should be similar, which is a string that is YYYY-MM-DD. When we look at the value of `inputs.date` bound with `v-model="inputs.date"` on a date `<input/>`, we should see the selected date in that format.

Listing 6-4 shows how to bind to the date input and Figure 6-3 shows how it looks in the browser.

Listing 6-4. Using v-model with an Input Type Date

```
<h4>Date</h4>
<input type="date" v-model="inputs.date" />
<p>
    <strong>Date:</strong> {{inputs.date}}
</p>
```

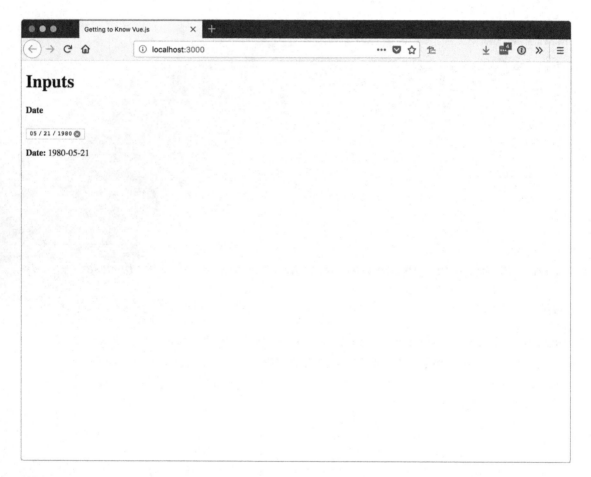

Figure 6-3. *Using v-model with an input type date with its output in the browser*

Password

Passwords bind the same as a text `<input/>` does. The only difference is that you can't see what is being typed. Listing 6-5 shows `v-model` with a password type `<input/>` and Figure 6-4 shows it in the browser if we type `"Getting to Know Vue.js"` in the `<input/>`.

Listing 6-5. Using v-model with a Password Input

```
<h4>Password</h4>
<input type="password" v-model="inputs.password" />
<p>
    <strong>Password:</strong> {{inputs.password}}
</p>
```

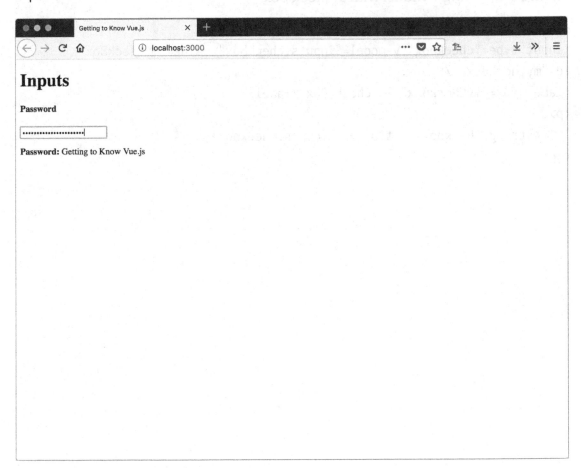

Figure 6-4. *Using v-model with a password input displayed in the browser*

Caution   If you are going to collect user passwords, do not send them in an unsecure manner over the Internet.

Check Boxes

A check box is the epitome of yes or no, true or false... okay, it's really just true or false. What form would be complete without a check box? Using v-model with a check box is the same as using the other `<input v-model="inputs.checkbox" />`.

Listing 6-6 shows how it's set up and Figure 6-5 shows the results of checking the check box.

Listing 6-6. Using v-model with a Check Box

```
<h4>Checkbox</h4>
<input type="checkbox" v-model="inputs.checkbox" value="myCheckBox"
id="myCheckBox" />
<label for="myCheckBox">My Check Box</label>
<p>
    <strong>Checkbox:</strong> {{inputs.checkbox}}
</p>
```

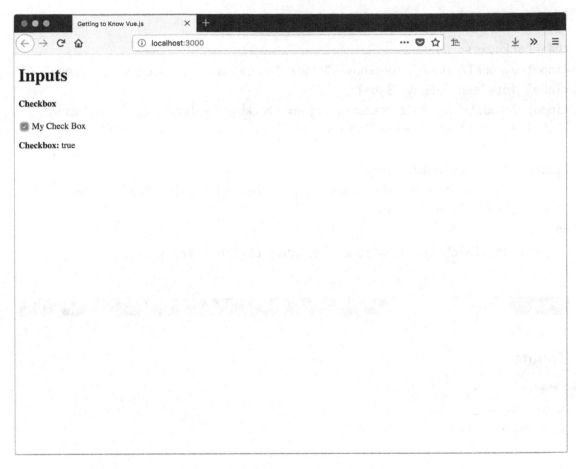

Figure 6-5. *Using v-model with a check box in the browser*

Groups of Check Boxes

What could be better than one check box? A group of check boxes! With Vue we can bind more than one check box to the same `data` property. If we have the `data` property as an array, Vue will push the value of the check box onto the array as it is selected.

In Listing 6-7 we use the `checkboxes` property that we initialized as an array in Listing 6-1. In Figure 6-6, we will select the check boxes for Miny and Enny and we should see them output in the order they are selected.

Listing 6-7. Using v-model with Multiple Check Boxes

```
<h4>Checkboxes</h4>
<input v-model="inputs.checkboxes" type="checkbox" value="eeny" id="eeny" />
<label for="eeny">Enny</label>
<input v-model="inputs.checkboxes" type="checkbox" value="meeny" id="meeny" />
<label for="meeny">Meenny</label>
<input v-model="inputs.checkboxes" type="checkbox" value="miny" id="miny" />
<label for="miny">Miny</label>
<input v-model="inputs.checkboxes" type="checkbox" value="mo" id="mo" />
<label for="mo">Mo</label>
<p>
    <strong>Checkboxes:</strong> {{inputs.checkboxes}}
</p>
```

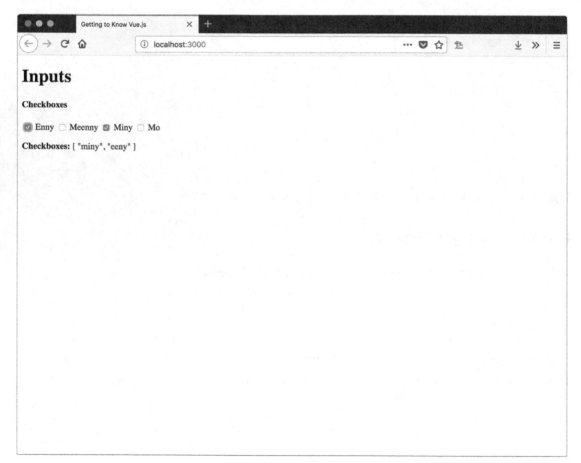

Figure 6-6. *Using v-model with multiple check boxes with Miny and Enny checked*

Radio Buttons

Radio buttons allow you to present the users with a selection of options similar to a group of check boxes, but the user can choose only one. Each radio button will be bound via the v-model to the same `backing data` property using v-model="inputs.radios" as the binding attribute.

Listing 6-8 shows four radio buttons and displays the value of the selected one beneath. You can see the results of selecting Go Joe! in Figure 6-7.

Listing 6-8. Using v-model with Radio Buttons

```
<h4>Radios</h4>
<input v-model="inputs.radios" type="radio" value="rollout" id="rollout" />
<label for="rollout">Autobots, transform and roll out!</label>
<br>
<input v-model="inputs.radios" type="radio" value="decepticons-retreat"
id="retreat" />
<label for="retreat">Decepticons, retreat!</label>
<br>
<input v-model="inputs.radios" type="radio" value="go-joe" id="go-joe" />
<label for="go-joe">Go Joe!</label>
<br>
<input v-model="inputs.radios" type="radio" value="cobra-retreat"
id="cobraretreat" />
<label for="cobraretreat">Cobra retreat. RETREAT!</label>
<p>
    <strong>Radios:</strong> {{inputs.radios}}
</p>
```

Figure 6-7. *Using v-model with radio buttons, with Go Joe! selected in the browser*

Preset Radio Buttons

We can also set a preset value for the user by setting the value of the backing property to the same value as one of the radio buttons. Listing 6-9 is essentially the same as Listing 6-8, but we use the `radiosPreset` property as the backing property that contains `rollout` as the value. When we load the page in Figure 6-8, Autobots, transform and roll out! will be selected for us.

Listing 6-9. Setting a Preset Value for Radio Buttons

```
<h4>Radios Preset</h4>
<input v-model="inputs.radiosPreset" type="radio" value="rollout"
id="rollout" />
<label for="rollout">Autobots, transform and roll out!</label>
```

```
<br>
<input v-model="inputs.radiosPreset" type="radio" value="decepticons-
retreat" id="retreat" />
<label for="retreat">Decepticons, retreat!</label>
<br>
<input v-model="inputs.radiosPreset" type="radio" value="go-joe" id="go-joe" />
<label for="go-joe">Go Joe!</label>
<br>
<input v-model="inputs.radiosPreset" type="radio" value="cobra-retreat"
id="cobraretreat" />
<label for="cobraretreat">Cobra retreat. RETREAT!</label>
<p>
    <strong>Radios:</strong> {{inputs.radiosPreset}}
</p>
```

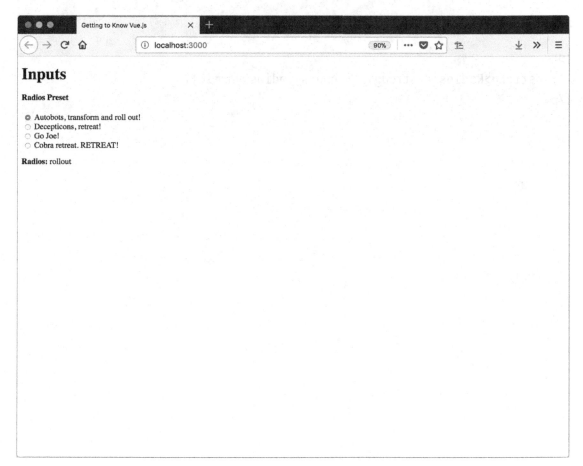

Figure 6-8. *Preset radio buttons upon first page load*

Radio Buttons: Dynamic Options

Creating radio buttons from a list of options may be required as the options could come from the server. In Listing 6-10, we will use v-for to create a radio button for each option in the radiosDynamicOptions array.

Listing 6-10. Creating Radio Buttons Dynamically

```
<h4>Radios Dynamic Options</h4>
<template v-for="(option, index) in inputs.radiosDynamicOptions">

    <input v-model="inputs.radiosDynamic" type="radio"
    v-bind:value="option.value" v-bind:id="option.value" />
    <label v-bind:for="option.value">{{option.label}}</label>
    <br v-if="index < inputs.radiosDynamicOptions.length">

</template>

<p>
    <strong>Radios:</strong> {{inputs.radiosDynamic}}
</p>
```

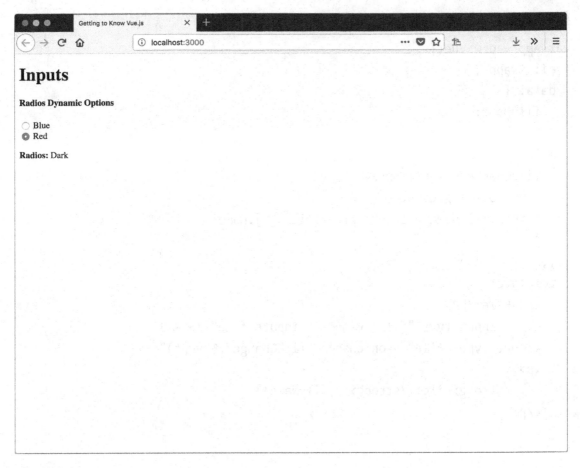

Figure 6-9. *Radio buttons created dynamically*

File

With file inputs, you cannot use `v-model`. To access the selected value, the `change` event will have to be used with `v-on`. Listing 6-11 shows how we use the event file `<input/>`'s change event to get the filename.

Listing 6-11. Using the Change Event for File Input

```
var app = new Vue({
  el: '#app',
  data: {
    fileName: "
  },
  methods: {
    fileChanged: function(event) {
      console.log(event);
      this.fileName = event.target.files[0].name;
    }
  },
  template: `
    <h4>File</h4>
    <!-- <input type="file" v-model="inputs.file" /> -->
    <input type="file" v-on:change="fileChanged($event)" />
    <p>
        <strong>File:</strong> {{fileName}}
    </p>
  `
});
```

Figure 6-10 shows the results of using our File input app after selecting a file called cover.png.

Figure 6-10. *Using the change event on a file input*

Hidden

Since we are using Vue and make the browser perform a full-page post to the server for form submission, this would mean that the users would have to wait for our app to load again. We won't use hidden fields in this case. Any values we want to send can be added to our post to the server in JavaScript.

Textarea Elements

The <textarea> elements allow us to collect more verbose responses from the users. Using v-model with a <textarea> is straightforward, as you can see in Listing 6-12. We apply the white-space: pre-line; style to our output element to preserve the whitespace. In Figure 6-11, we can see that each word displays on a new line in our output. We type "Getting to Know Vue.js" and press Enter between each line.

Listing 6-12. Using v-model with a textarea

```
<h4>Text</h4>
<textarea v-model="text" cols="50" style="height: 200px;"></textarea>
<p style="white-space: pre-line;">
    {{text}}
</p>
```

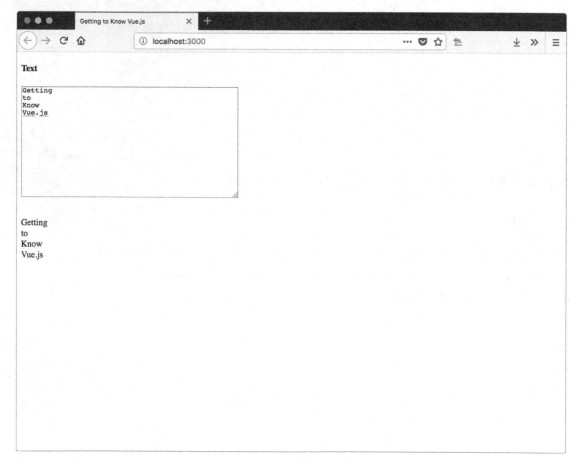

Figure 6-11. *Using v-model with a textarea in the browser*

Select

With a <select>, we bind to it and get the value that's selected. Listing 6-13 shows how to use v-model with a <select>, including having a recommended disabled options first. Providing a disabled first option helps the iOS not register a change event when the page loads and the first option becomes selected.

Listing 6-13. Using v-model with a select

```
<h4>Select</h4>
<select v-model="select">
    <option disabled value="">Select your Show
 </option>
    <option value="startrek">Star Trek</option>
    <option value="starwars">Star Wars</option>
    <option value="firefly">Firefly</option>
    <option value="drwho">Dr. Who</option>
</select>
<p>
    <strong>Selected:</strong> {{select}}
</p>
```

Figure 6-12. *Using v-model with a select and an option selected*

Multiple Selects

Multiple selects behave similarly to using multiple check boxes with the same backing property. The selected values get added as an array. Listing 6-14 uses `multiselect` with `v-model` and Figure 6-13 shows the results of selecting the second and fourth options.

Listing 6-14. Using v-model with a Multiselect

```
<h4>Multi-Select</h4>
<select v-model="multiSelect" multiple>
    <option value="startrek">Star Trek</option>
    <option value="starwars">Star Wars</option>
    <option value="firefly">Firefly</option>
```

```
    <option value="drwho">Dr. Who</option>
</select>
<p>
    <strong>Multi-Selected:</strong> {{multiSelect}}
</p>
```

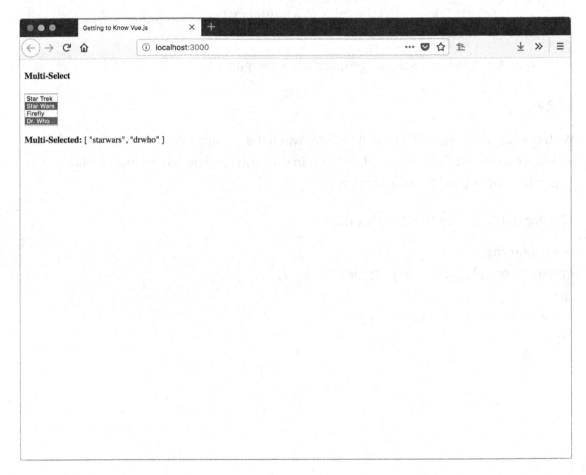

Figure 6-13. *Using v-model with a select and two options selected*

Modifiers

Vue provides us with three modifiers to use with inputs:

- .lazy: Uses the change event instead of the input event to update the data model.

- .number: Tries to cast the value to a number when assigning it to the data model.

- .trim: Removes the whitespace when assigning to the data model.

Lazy

With the .lazy modifier, the model updates when the change event occurs. To see this in action, you can use Listing 6-15 and view it in the browser. The output will display like in Figure 6-14 after you leave the input box.

Listing 6-15. Using the .lazy Modifier

```
<h4>Lazy</h4>
<input v-model.lazy="lazy" type="text" />
<p>
    <strong>Lazy:</strong> {{lazy}}
</p>
```

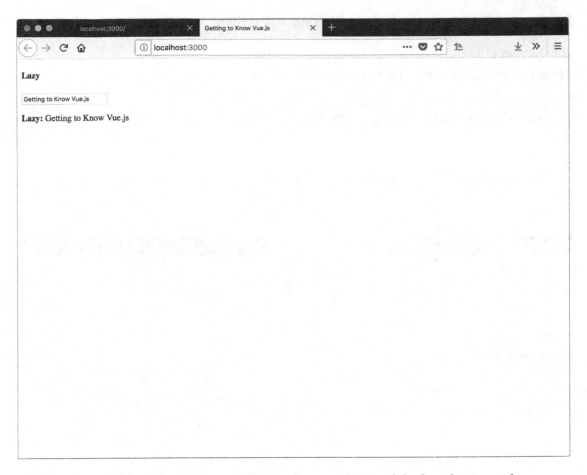

Figure 6-14. *Using the .lazy modifier to change the model after the input loses focus and fires a change event*

Number

The number modifier casts the value of the input to a number and we can use it on `<input/>`s with the type of number. In Listing 6-16, we use .number to cast our text input to a number. In Figure 6-15 you can see the output and the results of using `typeof` on our data backing fields.

Listing 6-16. Using .number Modifier on a Text Field

```
<h4>Number</h4>
<input v-model.number="number" type="text" />
<p>
    <strong>Number:</strong> {{number}}
</p>
<p>
    <strong>Type of Number:</strong> {{typeof number}}
</p>
```

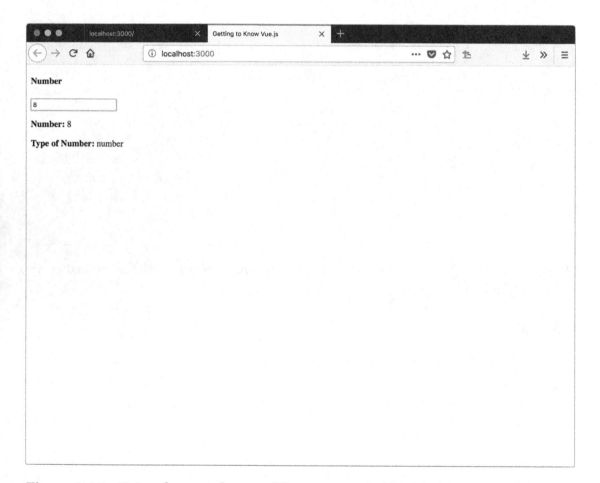

Figure 6-15. *Using the .number modifier on a text field with the output of the value and the typeof when the number 8 is entered*

Trim

The .trim modifier is used to remove the whitespace from the beginning and end of the value before updating the data model. Listing 6-17 show this effect by surrounding the output with quotes so we can see how much whitespace is at the beginning and end of the value. We also have an input with output that does not apply the trim modifier, so we can see how that behaves.

In Figure 6-16, we enter " Vue.js. " (that's five spaces before and five after Vue.js) into both inputs. In the No Trim input, you can see the space between Vue.js and the quotation marks. There is no space in the Trim output.

Listing 6-17. Using the .trim Modifier

```
<h4>No Trim</h4>
<input v-model="noTrim" type="text" />
<p>
    <strong>No Trim:</strong> "{{noTrim}}"
</p>

<h4>Trim</h4>
<input v-model.trim="trim" type="text" />
<p>
    <strong>Trim:</strong> "{{trim}}"
</p>
```

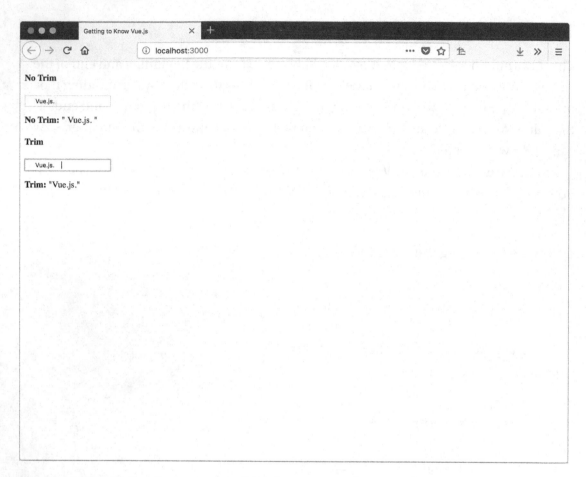

Figure 6-16. *Using the .trim modifier by entering " Vue.js. " into both inputs*

Styling

Providing users feedback about their actions usually takes on the form of changing the way things look on the page. The user enters invalid data in a form field, so something turns red. The user selects a drop-down menu and the menu drops down. Some of this could be accomplished with v-show and v-if, but it would feel abrupt. Using CSS properties and classes can provide a way to use animation and generally provide more options besides hiding and showing an element.

We look at applying CSS style properties and classes. If you would like to learn more about CSS, I recommend *CSS Mastery,* 3rd ed. Edition, by Andy Budd and Emil Björklund.

Inline Styles

Binding to inline styles allow us to directly assign values to CSS properties. We use syntax similar to binding to other attributes, as discussed in Chapter 2, but we use a JavaScript object we define in the expression. The property names can either be camel case or kebab case. If you use kebab case, you will need to use quotes. The value we assign each property will be the value assigned to the CSS property we used as the property name.

In Listing 6-18, we use the camel case name of fontSize to specify that we are setting the font size. For its value, we use a property from our Vue instance and append px to it, since we want to use pixels.

In Figure 6-17, you can see that entering 35 into the input sets the font size on our <p>.

Listing 6-18. Binding CSS Styles with an Inline Object

```
<h4>Dynamic Font Size</h4>
<input type="number" v-model.number="fontSize" />
<p v-bind:style="{fontSize: fontSize + 'px'}">
    Getting to Know Vue.js
</p>
```

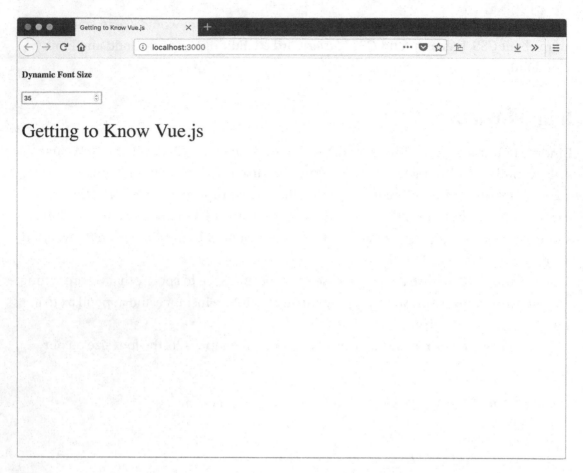

Figure 6-17. *Binding CSS styles with an inline object and setting the font size to 35*

Style Objects

Rather than defining the object we want to use for a style in the expression, we can define it as a data property. This way we can assign the whole object. We don't have to worry about defining our object as a string, as we can get proper syntax highlighting in the JavaScript editor.

In Listing 6-19, we bind the input to the same backing data property, `fontsize`, but we will add a watch to it so when it changes we can set the value of `fontSize` on our `fontSizeObject`. We will bind `fontSizeObject` to our `style` property.

Figure 6-18 shows the results with the input set to 25.

Listing 6-19. Using an Object to Set Styles

```
var app = new Vue({
  el: '#app',
  data: {
    fontSize: 0,
    fontSizeObject: { fontSize: '0px' }
  },
  watch: {
    fontSize: function() {
      this.fontSizeObject.fontSize = this.fontSize + 'px';
    }
  },
  template: `
<div>
  <h4>Dynamic Font Size with an object</h4>
  <input type="number" v-model.number="fontSize" />
  <p v-bind:style="fontSizeObject">
      Getting to Know Vue.js
  </p>
</div>
  `
});
```

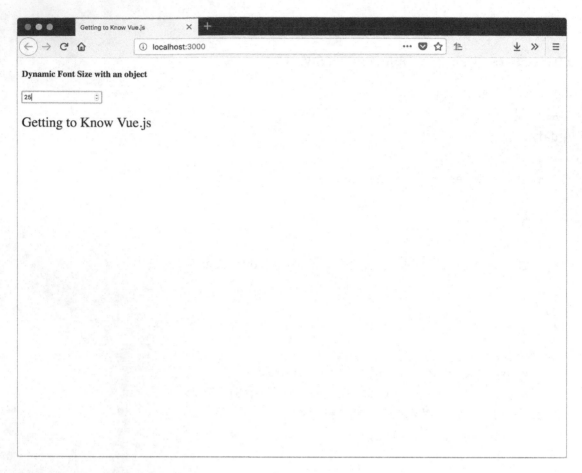

Figure 6-18. *Using an object to set styles with the input value set to 25*

The other thing you can do with the `style` object is use an array to bind more than one.

We will add the following property to our data model: `fontColorObject: { color: 'red' }`. We will add it to our `style` property with `fontSizeObject`, as in an array. Listing 6-20 shows the whole app and Figure 6-19 shows it with the font size set to 40.

Listing 6-20. Binding an Array of Objects to the Style Property

```
var app = new Vue({
  el: '#app',
  data: {
    fontSize: 0,
    fontSizeObject: { fontSize: '0px' },
    fontColorObject: { color: 'red' }
  },
  watch: {
    fontSize: function() {
      this.fontSizeObject.fontSize = this.fontSize + 'px';
    }
  },
  template: `
  <div>
    <h4>Dynamic Font Size with an object</h4>
    <input type="number" v-model.number="fontSize" />
    <p v-bind:style="[fontSizeObject, fontColorObject]">
        Getting to Know Vue.js
    </p>
  </div>
  `
});
```

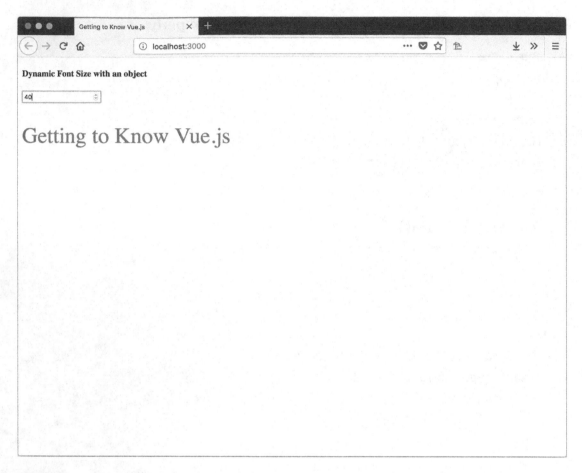

Figure 6-19. *Binding an array of objects to the style property with the font size set to 40*

Classes

Binding styles can make for a lot of hand-crafted work and makes it more difficult to reuse the look you have achieved. Thankfully we can also bind CSS classes.

To bind a CSS class, we use the `v-bind:class` directive on the element we want the class to be applied to. We provide it an object in the expression that has the name of the CSS class we want applied as property names and the condition that evaluates to `true` or `false` as the value. If we wanted to always apply a class, we could check if true equals true, as shown in Listing 6-21.

One Class

Listing 6-21. Binding a CSS Class

```
v-bind:class="{ cssClass : true == true }"
```

Note   The CSS class name can be in camel case or in kebab case. To use kebab case, you need to use quotation marks around the property name.

Listing 6-22 shows the CSS class, `error`, as defined in the head of our HTML. It turns the color red and adds a red solid border when applied to an element.

Listing 6-22. CSS error Class

```
<style>
    .error {
        color: red;
        border: red 3px solid;
    }
</style>
```

In Listing 6-23, we have our Vue app defined with two data properties, `input` and `inputError`, and a watch on input to set the value of `inputError`, depending on if the value of `input` is a number. Figure 6-20 shows the results of entering "word" into the input.

Listing 6-23. Binding a CSS Class to Evaluate a Data Property

```
var app = new Vue({
  el: '#app',
  data: {
    input: ",
    inputError: null
  },
```

```
  watch: {
    input: function() {
      var results = parseInt(this.input);
      if (isNaN(results)) {
        this.inputError = true;
      } else {
        this.inputError = false;
      }
    }
  },
  template: `
<div>
  <h4>One CSS Class Bound</h4>
  <input
          type="text"
          v-model="input"
          v-bind:class="{ error : inputError }" />
</div>
`

});
```

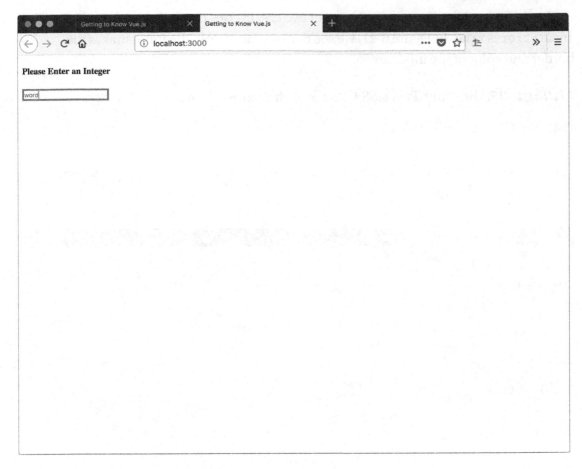

Figure 6-20. *Entering "word" into our input*

Multiple Classes

We can also use the object syntax to bind multiple CSS classes to an element by adding two or more properties with evaluation conditions of when to apply them.

Listing 6-24 shows our new CSS class, no-error. We will apply this when the input error is true.

Listing 6-24. No-error CSS Class

```
.no-error {
    color: green;
    border: green 3px solid;
}
```

119

Listing 6-25 shows how to apply one of two CSS classes depending on whether inputError is true. In Figure 6-21, we see that entering 5 into the input makes the border and color of the input green.

Listing 6-25. Binding Two CSS Classes to the Same Element

```
<h4>Two Classes Bound</h4>
<input type="text" v-model="input"
        v-bind:class="{ error : inputError, 'no-error' : inputError ==
        false }" />
```

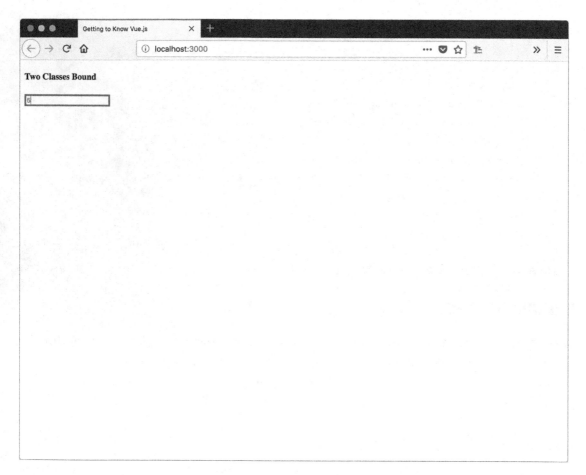

Figure 6-21. *Entering a valid input applies the no-error CSS class*

Multiple Classes with Arrays

We can also apply multiple CSS classes with an array. Listing 6-26 shows our `.active` class. Listing 6-27 shows the Vue app with two properties, with the values being the names of our CSS `.error` and `.active` classes. Figure 6-22 shows our oversized input with an error.

Listing 6-26. Our .active CSS Class

```
.active {
    font-size: 1.5em;
}
```

Listing 6-27. Binding Multiple CSS Classes with an Array

```
var app = new Vue({
  el: '#app',
  data: {
    activeClass: 'active',
    errorClass: 'error'
  },
  template: `
<div>
    <h4>CSS Classes in an Array</h4>
    <input
        type="text"
        v-model="input"
        v-bind:class="[activeClass, errorClass]" />

</div>
`
});
```

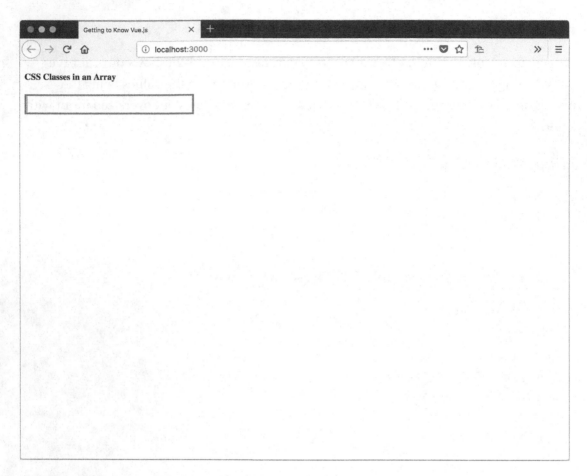

Figure 6-22. *Two CSS classes applied with an array*

You can also use the object expression syntax to dynamically apply a class in an array. Listing 6-28 shows how to accomplish this. One thing to note is that we are applying the "error" class name as a string, not a reference, to the data property that holds the same value.

Listing 6-28. Dynamically Applying a CSS Class as Part of an Array

```
<input
      type="text"
      v-model="input"
      v-bind:class="[{ 'error' : inputError }, activeClass]" />
```

Computed Classes

Declaring the logic on which CSS class to apply in the markup can get a little verbose. It makes things a little more difficult to read. We can get around that issue by using a computed property to create the object we bind to the class attribute.

To bind to a computed property, we provide the attribute the name v-bind:class="appliedCss". The real magic happens in our Vue instance.

In Listing 6-29, we have a computed property that always applies the active class and conditionally applies the error and no-error class depending on the value of inputError. If we enter "word" into our input, you can see the error class is applied in Figure 6-23. If we enter "4", the no-error class is applied, as shown in Figure 6-24.

Listing 6-29. Using a Computed Property to Apply CSS Classes

```
var app = new Vue({
  el: '#app',
  data: {
    input: ",
    inputError: null
  },
  watch: {
    input: function() {
      var results = parseInt(this.input);
      if (isNaN(results)) {
        this.inputError = true;
      } else {
        this.inputError = false;
      }
    }
  },
  computed: {
    appliedCss: function() {
      return {
        active: true,
        error: this.inputError,
        'no-error': this.inputError === false
```

```
      };
    }
  },
  template: `
<div>
    <h4>Using Computed Properties for CSS classes</h4>
    <input type="text" v-model="input" v-bind:class="appliedCss" />
</div>
    `

});
```

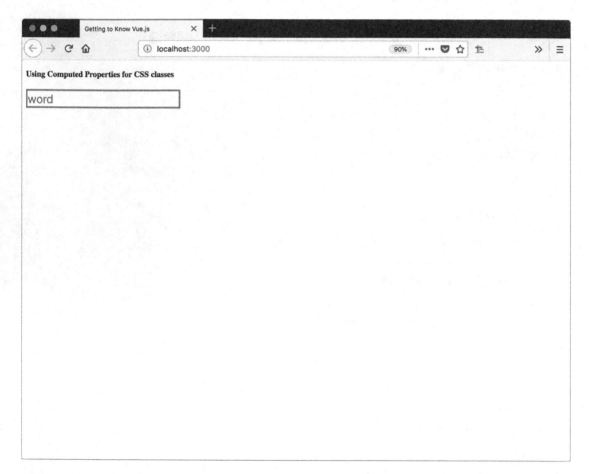

Figure 6-23. *Applying a computed property as a CSS class with "word" as the input*

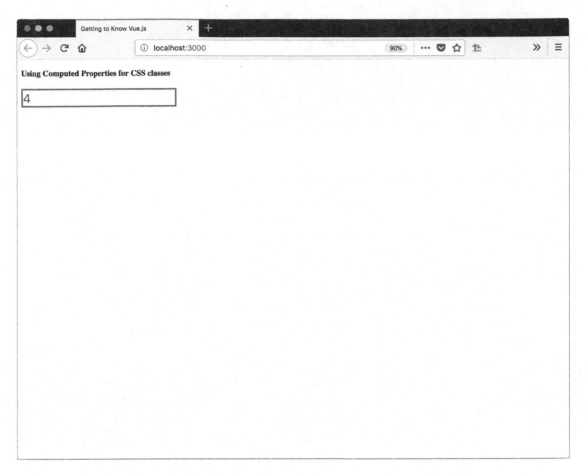

Figure 6-24. *Applying a computed property as a CSS class with "4" as the input*

Summary

In this chapter, we learned about binding to inputs, styles, and CSS classes. With Vue handling the many different forms of inputs, getting the value the user enters requires `v-model`. Vue provides many options for binding CSS styles and classes, which allow us to bind with inline syntax, to an object, to an array, and even use computed properties.

CHAPTER 7

State Management

Every application has some data to manage in the form of values to keep track of related to the user's choices or the information that is being displayed. To further complicate things, we could be using the same data across multiple instances of Vue. Handling this is called *state management*. We will take a look at three ways to manage state with Vue: a simple data object, a do-it-yourself data store, and a state management library called Vuex.

Simple Data Objects

The most basic way to manage and share data is with a simple JavaScript object that has some properties with values. This object is then passed into multiple Vue instances to share access to the same values.

Listing 7-1 shows an example of this rudimentary sharing of data.

Listing 7-1. Basic Data Sharing

```
var sharedData = {
  value: 1
};

var app1 = new Vue({
  el: '#app1',
  data: {
    shared: sharedData,
    private: {}
  },
```

© Brett Nelson 2018
B. Nelson, *Getting to Know Vue.js*, https://doi.org/10.1007/978-1-4842-3781-6_7

```
  template: `
    <h1>App 1 Shared Value: {{shared.value}}</h1>
  `
});
var app2 = new Vue({
  el: '#app2',
  data: {
    shared: sharedData,
    private: {}
  },
  methods: {
    increase: function() {
      this.$data.shared.value++;
    },
    decrease: function() {
      sharedData.value--;
    }
  },
  template: `
    <div>
      <h1>App 2 Shared Value: {{shared.value}}</h1>
      <button v-on:click="increase">+</button>
      <button v-on:click="decrease">-</button>
    </div>
  `
});
```

You can see we have a separate JavaScript object that has one property, `value`. This object is then used as the data property for two different Vue instances, `app1` and `app2`.

In `app2`, we have two buttons to change the values of the `sharedData` object through an `increase` and `decrease` method. In the `increase` method, we use the Vue instances reference to the original data object that was stored when the instance was created with through `this.$data`. In the `decrease` method, we directly manipulate the JavaScript object that was used as the value for the data property.

In Figure 7-1, you can see that clicking the + button three times results in the values of both Vue instances being updated.

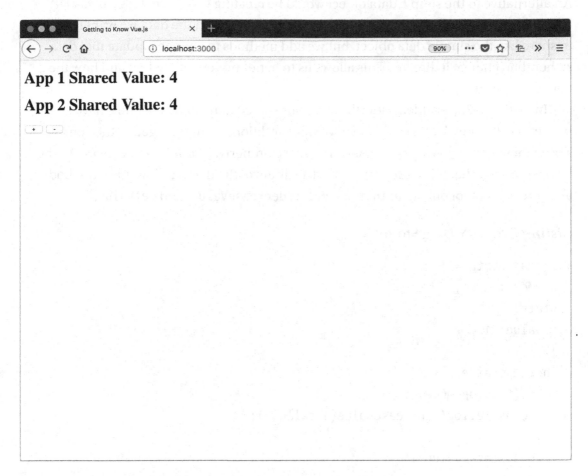

Figure 7-1. *Basic data sharing updating two Vue instances*

This looks like a working solution. However, the thing is, as your application gets more complex, it will get more and more difficult to verify that the shared data is being changed properly, since every Vue instance it is shared with can change it directly.

DIY Data Store

An alternative to the simple data object would be creating your own; let's call it a DIY (Do It Yourself) data store. We use a JavaScript object to hold the data we want to be able to share like the simple data object, but we add methods to change/update that data rather than change it directly. This allows us to better understand when and how the data is being changed.

In Listing 7-2, we added a few things to our shared data object. We now have a property called devMode to indicate if we want additional things logged to the console. The values we are sharing now reside in a state property. In our Vue instances, it's the state property that we use for our shared attribute of the data. And we have methods to alter the value(s) of our state: increaseValue, decreaseValue, and setValue.

Listing 7-2. DIY Data Store

```javascript
var sharedData = {
  devMode: true,
  state: {
    value: 1
  },
  increaseValue() {
    if (this.devMode) {
      console.log('increaseValue() called');
    }
    this.state.value++;
  },
  decreaseValue() {
    if (this.devMode) {
      console.log('decreaseValue() called');
    }
    this.state.value--;
  },
  setValue(newValue) {
    if (this.devMode) {
      console.log('setValue() called with newValue: ', newValue);
    }
```

```
      this.state.value = newValue;
   }
};
```

In the methods to alter the state, we check if devMode is true. If it is, we log a message to the console. We would want to set this to false or remove the devMode property before deploying it to production. Once it's in production, we would be able to turn dev mode on using the browser dev tools console and setting sharedData.devMode = true manually.

To update the data in sharedData, we call the method off of the sharedData object that corresponds to the action we want to take. Want to increase the value? Call sharedData.increaseValue(). Want to set the value to 1? Call sharedData.setValue(1). You can see this in Listing 7-3.

Listing 7-3. Consuming a DIY Data Store

```
var app1 = new Vue({
  el: '#app1',
  data: {
    shared: sharedData.state,
    private: {}
  },
  template: `
    <h1>App 1 Shared Value: {{shared.value}}</h1>

  `
});

var app2 = new Vue({
  el: '#app2',
  data: {
    shared: sharedData.state,
    private: {}
  },
  methods: {
    increase: function() {
      sharedData.increaseValue();
    },
```

```
    decrease: function() {
      sharedData.decreaseValue();
    },
    reset: function() {
      sharedData.setValue(1);
    }
  },
  template: `
    <div>
      <h1>App 2 Shared Value: {{shared.value}}</h1>
      <button v-on:click='increase'>+</button>
      <button v-on:click='decrease'>-</button>
      <button v-on:click='reset'>reset</button>
    </div>
    `

});
```

You can see that instead of changing the data in our Vue instance, we are using the increase, decrease, and reset methods to call the methods on the sharedData.

This makes things a little more manageable as we have one place where all the data changes occur.

Vuex

Having learned about the DIY data store, you are probably wonder what other options could be needed for managing state. Vuex is a library maintained by the Vue team that provides state management along with some additional treats or features. The official Vue dev tool plugin enables Vuex to perform *time travel* debugging along with importing and exporting the state. Vuex is designed to act as the application state for all Vue components of your application.

Install

Before we can start to use Vuex, we need to install it.

CDN or Self Hosted

If you are not using a module system to manage dependencies, you can reference Vuex from the CDN (content delivery network) or download a copy to host on the same server as your app. Use the address `https://unpkg.com/vuex` for the latest version.

When using it as a CDN, I recommend using a versioned reference. This is so nothing unexpectedly changes while it's in production by adding the version number at the end or the URL. If you want to use version 3.0.1, the URL would be `https://unpkg.com/vuex@3.0.1`.

When you add the `<script>` element to reference Vuex, add it after the Vue `<script>` and Vuex will self-register for use.

Note   If you need to add Vuex before Vue to your page you can still register it for use with `Vue.use(Vuex);`.

NPM and Yarn

If you are using NPM or Yarn to manage your apps dependencies it can be installed by the package of the same name: vuex. So, for NPM it would be `npm install vuex –save` and for Yarn it would be `yarn add vuex`. Then in the code it will have to be imported from the module system, like in Listing 7-4, before you tell Vue to use it.

Listing 7-4. Importing Vuex for Use

```
import Vue from 'vue';
import Vuex from 'vuex';

Vue.use(Vuex);
```

Promise

Vuex does require that the browser supports promises. If you plan on supporting browsers that don't have an implementation of promises, you'll need a polyfill.

One promise library that works with Vuex is `es6-promise`. It can be referenced or downloaded from a CDN at `https://cdn.jsdelivr.net/npm/es6-promise@4/dist/es6-promise.auto.js`. It can also be installed with NPM using `npm install es6-promise -save` or with Yarn, using `yarn add es6-promise`. Be sure to include an `import` statement for the polyfill where you are using Vuex `import 'es6-promise/auto';`.

Note   Vuex solves some of the more complicated problems, so to demonstrate it better, we need a more complicated example. We will be using the Star Wars API, `https://swapi.co/`, to get a list of star ships and then load the pilots of a selected ship with the Axios library at `https://github.com/axios/axios`.

Options

With everything set up for use, we can get on with configuring our instance of Vuex. To do that, we should probably have an understanding of what properties we pass in when creating a new instance of Vuex.

State

The `state` property is similar to the `state` property we used in our DIY data store. It contains all the data we are sharing with Vuex. Since our Vue apps will only have a single Vuex instance, the state is a single JavaScript object that contains the state for the entire app. Listing 7-5 shows a basic store.

Listing 7-5. State Setup

```
state: {
  ship: {},
  ships: { count: 0, results: [] },
  pilots: []
},
```

Getters

Getters offer a way to consolidate results that is based on the data in the store. One way to think of a getter is as a computed property that is exposed through the store, thereby allowing it to be reused in multiple Vue components. In the vein of computed properties, the results of most getters are cached.

A getter function receives two parameters: state and getters. The state function is used to access the values of the store. The getters function can be used to combine results of other getters, thereby allowing us to build more complicated results in smaller portions.

Listing 7-6 shows a getter that returns a filtered array of ships that have a starship_ class of Starfighter. We then have a second getter that returns the number of Starfighters in our current list.

Listing 7-6. Two Getters, One That Returns a List of Only Starfighter and One That Returns the Number of Starfighters

```
onlyStarFighters: function(state) {
  return state.ships.results.filter(function(ship) {
    return ship.starship_class === 'Starfighter';
  });
},
onlyStarFightersCount: function(state, getters) {
  return getters.onlyStarFighters.length;
},
```

A getter can return the results of some logic, like a formatted string, a new number, or a function. When a function is returned, it can be used to pass in a value, such as an ID to search for from the store or some other value to get the results of the getter.

Listing 7-7 shows a getter that returns a function. That function accepts the url parameter and then returns the ship with that url.

Listing 7-7. A Getter Returning a Function That Accepts a Parameter to Evaluate the Result

```
setShip: function(state) {
  return function(url) {
    return state.ships.results.find(function(ship) {
      return ship.url === url;
    });
  };
}
```

Note   Getters that return a function are evaluated every time they are accessed.

Mutations

The only way to change the value of the store is through a mutation. A mutation consists of a string type and a handler function. One way to think of the type is that it's like the name for the handler. The handler is a function that accepts at least one parameter, state, and can have a second parameter called payload. If multiple values need to be passed to the mutation, we can use an object.

Since every mutation is logged to track changes, all mutations must be synchronous. If a mutation needs to perform an action that is asynchronous due to using a callback or promise, the logic should probably be moved to an action. More on actions next.

Listing 7-8 has four mutations—setShips sets the ships property of state, setShip sets the ship of state, clearPilots replaces the contents of the pilots property of state with an empty array, and addPilot adds a pilot to the pilots property of state.

Listing 7-8. Mutation Examples

```
mutations: {
  setShips: function(state, payload) {
    state.ships = payload.newShips;
  },
  setShip: function(state, payload) {
    state.ship = payload.newShip;
```

```
  },
  clearPilots: function(state) {
    state.pilots = [];
  },
  addPilot: function(state, payload) {
    state.pilots.push(payload.newPilot);
  }
},
```

To invoke, or call, a mutation, we call `commit` on the `store` object. When we call `commit`, we can pass it the type, or name, of the mutation to call and a payload, or we can pass it an object that has a property named `type`. The rest of the object will be the payload. We can see both ways of calling `commit` in Listing 7-9.

We can call this on the `store` object that is stored as a JavaScript object or we can call it from our Vue instances reference to the store that was passed in when we created our instance.

Listing 7-9 shows how to call `commit` on the store using the global JavaScript store variable, the reference from the Vue instance, along with passing a payload. It also shows how to pass an object that specifies the type.

Listing 7-9. Calling commit

```
search: function(event) {
  store.dispatch('search', { searchText: event.target.value });
},
viewShip: function(url) {
  this.$store.dispatch({ type: 'setShip', url: url });
}
```

Actions

Sometimes we need to perform a task that is not synchronous, so a mutation won't work. That's where actions come in. An action can be asynchronous. Any task that might require a callback or a wait period such as calling a server should be an action.

When the asynchronous task is done, we will be able to call commit with the results. This will preserve the transaction history of our Vuex and still allow us all those fun calls to servers.

Actions follow the same format as mutations with a string type, or name, and a handler function. The handler function accepts two parameters: context and payload. The context parameter contains the same properties and methods as the store does in a mutation, allowing us to access the state and commit mutations.

To call, or invoke, an action, we follow the same format as when committing a mutation, except we call dispatch on the store.

Listing 7-10 shows three actions: search to search for ships, setShip to set the current ship, and getPilots to get the pilots once the ship is set. In the setPilots action, we also use the dispatch method to call getPilots.

Listing 7-10. Action Examples

```
actions: {
  search: function(context, payload) {
    axios
      .get(`https://swapi.co/api/starships/?search=${payload.searchText}`)
      .then(response => {
        context.commit('setShips', { newShips: response.data });
      });
  },
  setShip: function(context, payload) {
    context.commit('clearPilots');
    context.commit('setShip', {
      newShip: context.getters.setShip(payload.url)
    });
```

```
    context.dispatch('getPilots', { urls: context.state.ship.pilots });
  },
  getPilots: function(context, payload) {
    payload.urls.forEach(function(url) {
      axios.get(url).then(response => {
        context.commit('addPilot', { newPilot: response.data });
      });
    });
  }
}
```

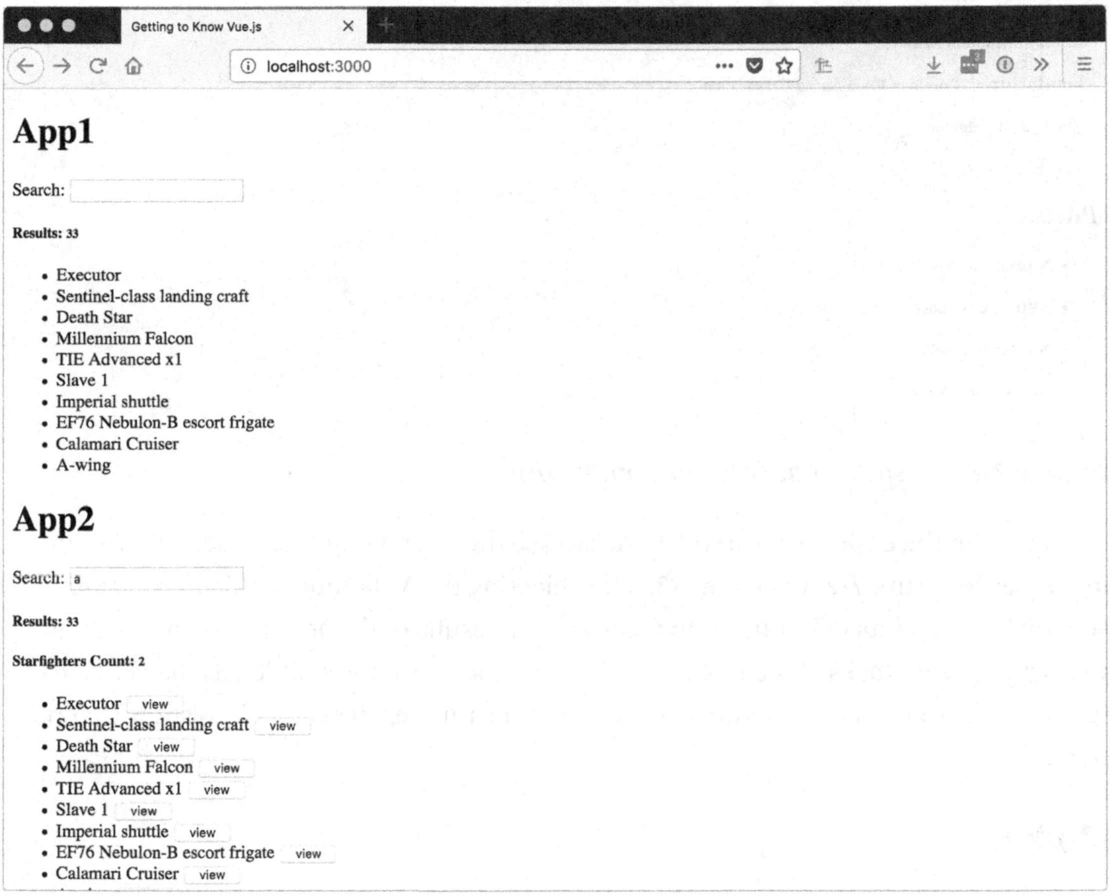

Figure 7-2. *Two Vue instances sharing data*

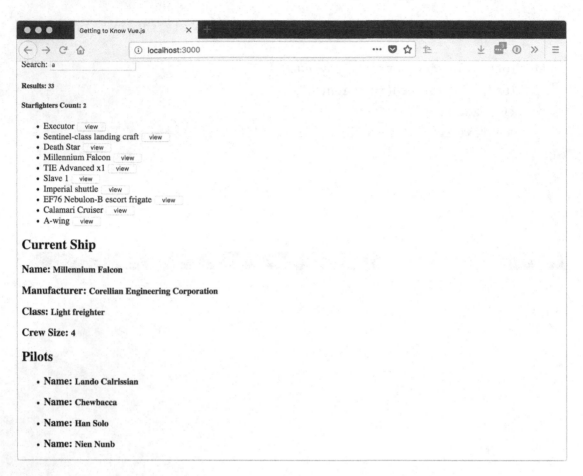

Figure 7-3. *Results of actions and mutations*

If we run the code we have so far, we can see the data being shared across two Vue instances in Figure 7-2. In Figure 7-3, after selecting the Millennium Falcon, we can see the lists of pilots below the ship details as the results of the actions and mutations performing their tasks. Watching it "live," you can see each pilot added as the HTTP call to the server returns the results for each one. Unfortunately it's difficult to show that part here.

Modules

After a few releases, any small app can start to get larger in scale. Managing larger data stores can become a bit of a challenge. To help us deal with this, Vuex allows us to declare a store in modules. Each module is like a mini-Vuex declaration with its own state, getters, mutations, and actions.

These modules allow us to break up our data store into manageable chucks the same way we would split up any larger programming issue into smaller, more manageable portions.

Basics

Using our example app that allows us to access ships and pilots from the Star Wars API, we can break our existing Vuex definition into two modules: ships and pilots.

Listing 7-11 shows our shipsModule with the state, getters, mutations, and actions that apply only to the ships. Listing 7-12 shows our pilotsModule with the state, getters, mutations, and actions that apply only to the pilots.

Listing 7-11. Ships Module Definition

```
var shipsModule = {
  state: {
    ship: {},
    ships: { count: 0, results: [] }
  },
  getters: {
    onlyStarFighters: function(state) {
      return state.ships.results.filter(function(ship) {
        return ship.starship_class === 'Starfighter';
      });
    },
    onlyStarFightersCount: function(state, getters) {
      return getters.onlyStarFighters.length;
    },
    setShip: function(state) {
      return function(url) {
        return state.ships.results.find(function(ship) {
          return ship.url === url;
        });
      };
    }
  },
  mutations: {
```

141

```
    setShips: function(state, payload) {
      state.ships = payload.newShips;
    },
    setShip: function(state, payload) {
      state.ship = payload.newShip;
    }
  },
  actions: {
    search: function(context, payload) {
      axios
        .get(`https://swapi.co/api/starships/?search=${payload.
        searchText}`)
        .then(response => {
          context.commit('setShips', { newShips: response.data });
        });
    },
    setShip: function(context, payload) {
      context.commit('clearPilots');
      context.commit('setShip', {
        newShip: context.getters.setShip(payload.url)
      });
      context.dispatch('getPilots', { urls: context.state.ship.pilots });
    }
  }
};
```

Listing 7-12. Pilots Module Definition

```
var pilotsModule = {
  state: {
    pilots: []
  },
  getters: {},
  mutations: {
    clearPilots: function(state) {
      state.pilots = [];
```

```
    },
    addPilot: function(state, payload) {
      state.pilots.push(payload.newPilot);
    }
  },
  actions: {
    getPilots: function(context, payload) {
      payload.urls.forEach(function(url) {
        axios.get(url).then(response => {
          context.commit('addPilot', { newPilot: response.data });
        });
      });
    }
  }
};
```

Looking at these module definitions, you might notice that they don't use Vuex at this point. They are plain JavaScript objects. To use these module definitions, we create a new Vuex store using the module's options. In the `modules` property we define each module with a property name and assign the definition as the value.

Listing 7-13 shows our new Vuex store using `shipsModule` and `pilotsModule`.

Listing 7-13. Using Module Definitions

```
var store = new Vuex.Store({
  modules: {
    ships: shipsModule,
    pilots: pilotsModule
  }
});
```

For the most part, this will make our app work the same as before we started using modules. The only change we have to make is where we reference the state in our computed properties.

Outside the module to access our state from `shipsModule`, we will now need to use `this.$store.state.ships` to get access to the `ships` state and use `this.$store.state.pilots` to access the `pilots` state.

Note   Inside the module we still use the `state` to access the current state
properties, as seen in Listings 7-11 and 7-12.

Listing 7-14 shows an update to our `app2` computed properties, which access the
`ships` and `pilots` states.

Listing 7-14. Accessing Module State

```
computed: {
  currentShip: function() {
    return this.$store.state.ships.ship;
  },
  ships: function() {
    return this.$store.state.ships.ships.results;
  },
  shipCount: function() {
    return this.$store.state.ships.ships.count;
  },
  starfightersCount: function() {
    return this.$store.getters.onlyStarFightersCount;
  },
  pilots: function() {
    return this.$store.state..pilots;
  }
},
```

After updating our computed properties, everything will work the same as before we
broke things out into modules.

Accessing RootState

In your actions and getters, you may need to access the main state of your data store to
get information from a different module. This is possible through a third parameter that
is passed in to both actions and getters called `rootState`.

In Listing 7-15, we use the rootState in a getter that returns a list of strings that say the current pilots name followed by "the pilot of" and the ship name by accessing the ship names through the rootState.

Listing 7-15. Using rootState to Access a Second Module State

```
pilotsWithShipName: function(state, getters, rootState) {
  return state.pilots.map(function(pilot) {
    return `${pilot.name} the pilot of ${rootState.ships.ship.name}`;
  });
}
```

Namespace

Since the modules we created, ships and pilots, didn't have much in the way of overlapping names of getters, actions, and mutations, I didn't feel the need to namespace the modules. At some point, you may need to specify which specific modules should handle an action, getter, or mutations.

To namespace a module, add namespaced: true as one of its properties and you're done... almost. Now to access the mutations from outside the module, you call commit('moduleName/mutationName'). To access an action, we call dispatch('moduleName/actionName'). And to access a getter, we have to use getters['moduleName/getterName']. Notice we are using the bracket notation to access the getter since JavaScript dot notation will not let us use the / special character.

Inside the module, we can use either the namespace method to access the mutations, actions, and getters or we can call them without the namespacing.

Listing 7-16 shows adding the namespaced: true property to our pilotsModule.

Listing 7-16. Namespaced Module

```
var pilotsModule = {
  namespaced: true,
  //everything else stays the same
}
```

Listing 7-17 shows how we access the clearPilots mutations and the getPilots action from the shipsModule now that the pilotsModule is using a namespace.

Listing 7-17. Accessing a Namespaced Module

```
setShip: function(context, payload) {
  context.commit('pilots/clearPilots');
  context.commit('setShip', {
    newShip: context.getters.setShip(payload.url)
  });
  context.dispatch('pilots/getPilots', { urls: context.state.ship.pilots
});
}
```

We can also decide to make an action globally available by registering it as such. To register an action as global, we change the definition of the action from a function to an object with two properties: `root` and `handler`. The `handler` property will be the function that we used to have assigned to the action. The `root` property will be set to `true`.

Listing 7-18 shows the `getPilots` action set as a global action.

Listing 7-18. Registering a Global Action

```
getPilots: {
  root: true,
  handler: function(context, payload) {
    payload.urls.forEach(function(url) {
      axios.get(url).then(response => {
        context.commit('addPilot', { newPilot: response.data });
      });
    });
  }
}
```

With a namespace module, our getters get a forth parameter, called `rootGetters`. We can use `rootGetters` to access getters from other modules, similar to the way we used our `rootState` parameter.

Listing 7-19 shows the `pilotsModule` getter for `pilotsWithShipName` using the `rootGetter` to get all the ships for a pilot.

Listing 7-19. Using rootGetters to Access Getters in Different Modules

```
pilotsWithShipName: function(state, getters, rootState, rootGetters) {
  return state.pilots.map(function(pilot) {
    return `${
      pilot.name
    } flies ${rootGetters.getShipsWithPilotId(pilot.url).length} number of
    the current ships`;
  });
}
```

Summary

In this chapter, we learned three ways we can manage the state of our application. A simple data object has some drawbacks in that there is no central way to maintain consistency of changes or to track where the changes are occurring. A DIY data store starts to add specific ways to manage changes to the data, thereby allowing for some support for tracking changes. Vuex offers a more robust method for tracking changes, including change history, but becomes a little more verbose when you're connecting it within your app.

CHAPTER 8

Using Components

It's not usually a good idea to get all your apps into one JavaScript file. With Vue we can use components to create reusable portions of our app and make it easier to maintain. In this chapter, we will learn how to create and use a custom Vue component, share data with components, use events, and use slots.

What Is a Component?

You might be wondering what a component is and why you should care. Both those questions are good things to figure out.

A component in the sense that we are going to be exploring is a custom element that we can define and reuse. We will define our components as little instances of Vue, but instead of calling new Vue for a full instance of Vue, we have to register them where needed. So, each component will have its version of most things that a Vue instance has except for an el property.

Most Vue applications end up being a collection of Vue components working together to display data and react to the user's interactions.

First Component

To make our fist component, we will use Vue.component to register the component. Think of registering the component as telling Vue about it so it will be available for use. We will pass in two parameters to register our component—a name for the component and a JavaScript object that contains all the options for it.

© Brett Nelson 2018

B. Nelson, *Getting to Know Vue.js*, https://doi.org/10.1007/978-1-4842-3781-6_8

The name for the component can be either kebab case, using hyphens to separate words and all lowercase like kebab-case, or PascalCase, using capital letters and no spaces to identify new words, like PascalCase. If we use kebab case, we will be able to use our component as a custom element by using its name as the element, like <our-custom-component>. If we use PascalCase, we will be able to use our component with the PascalCase version of the name, <OurCustomComponent>, or the kebab case version of the name, <our-custom-component>. Since using PascalCase is not valid HTML syntax, we cannot use it in a DOM template.

In Listing 8-1 we create our first component. It has the name OurHeader and creates an <h1> element that says App Header.

Listing 8-1. Creating Our First Custom Component

```
Vue.component('OurHeader', {
  template: `
    <h1>App Header</h1>
  `
});
```

In Listing 8-2, we add it to our app using both the kebab case and PascalCase methods.

Listing 8-2. Using Our First Custom Component

```
<our-header></our-header>

<OurHeader></OurHeader>
```

When we load our app, we should see two copies of our headers, as shown in Figure 8-1.

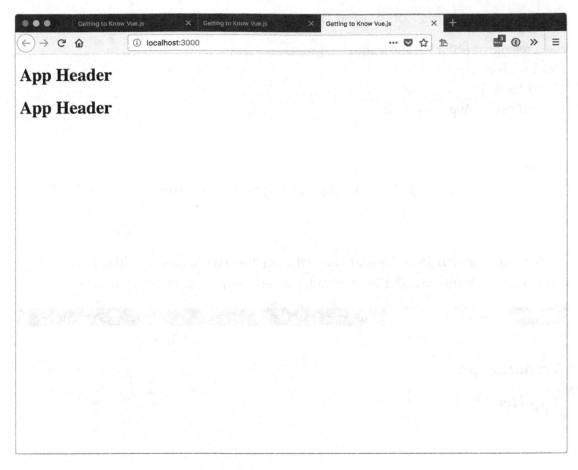

Figure 8-1. Our first component in use

Using Data

We might not want to have everything defined in markup; in our first component, we might feel it's important to move the text to the data of our component. Since a component is an instance of Vue, we can specify data that it contains.

The big point to note is that with components, data is defined as a function that returns an object instead of as an object. This is so that each instance of the component will have its own copy of the data, isolating it from the changes in instances of the component.

Listing 8-3 shows our second component, where we define the data as a function that returns an object. We also have a click event handler that reverses text.

151

Listing 8-3. Defining Component Data

```
Vue.component('OurSecondHeader', {
  data: function() {
    return {
      text: 'App Header 2'
    };
  },
  template: `
    <h1 v-on:click="text = text.split("").reverse().join("")">{{text}}</h1>
  `
});
```

If we add two OurSecondHeaders and click on the first one, we should see only the text of the first instance of OurSecondHeader reverse its text, as shown in Figure 8-2.

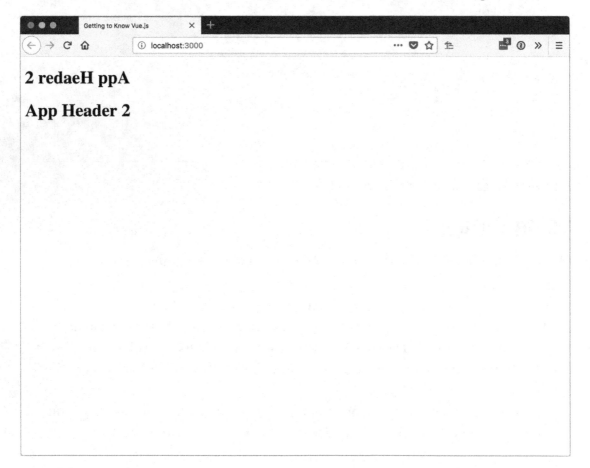

Figure 8-2. *Showing components isolated*

Passing Data with Props

Having a component that contains its own data is great, but most likely it would be nicer to pass data to the component from the parent component, so we could reuse it. With `props`, we can specify values that can be passed to the component.

Listing 8-4 shows how to declare a prop on a component using the `props` option and assign it an array of strings for the names of `props` to use. In this case, our array will have only one prop, `text`. We will use the value of `text` to set the text of our `<h1>` in the template.

Listing 8-4. Defining Props

```
Vue.component('OurThirdHeader', {
  props: ['text'],
  template: `
    <h1>{{text}}</h1>
  `
});
```

Now when we use our component, we can pass in the text to display in our component. Listing 8-5 shows a static assignment to the `text` prop. Static in this case means that the value is a literal string that is declared in the markup.

Listing 8-5. Assigning a Value to Our Text Prop

```
<OurThirdHeader text="App Header 3" />
```

This will display the results shown in Figure 8-3.

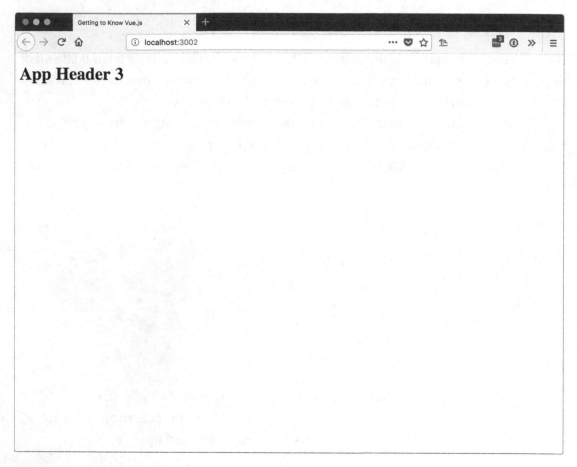

Figure 8-3. *Using props to pass values*

Rather than pass a static value to the text prop, we can bind to a value in the parent component. Listing 8-6 shows how to bind the value of appLabel from the parent component to the text prop with v-bind.

Listing 8-6. Binding Data to the text Prop

```
var app = new Vue({
  el: '#app',
  data: {
    appLabel: 'App'
  },
```

```
template: `
    <div>
      <OurThirdHeader v-bind:text="appLabel" />
    </div>
      `
});
```

Props also allows us to specify types and default values, determine whether they are required, and use validators. At a minimum, it is a good idea to specify a type. This can be done by assigning an object instead of an array to the props property. Each property of this object will be the name of a prop and the value will be the type that it supports.

Listing 8-7 shows how to specify a type for our text prop.

Listing 8-7. Specifying a Type for a Prop

```
Vue.component('OurFourthHeader', {
  props: {
    text: String
  },
  template: `
    <h1>{{text}}</h1>
      `
});
```

This will behave the same as when we didn't specify a type, but if we bind it to a value that is not a string, it will log an error to the developer console in the browser. This is helpful when developing components to remind the developer using the component what value types are expected.

Acceptable types to use when specifying the props type are the standard JavaScript object types:

- String
- Number
- Boolean
- Array
- Object

155

Figure 8-4 shows the results of binding the number 0 to OurFourthHeader's text prop.

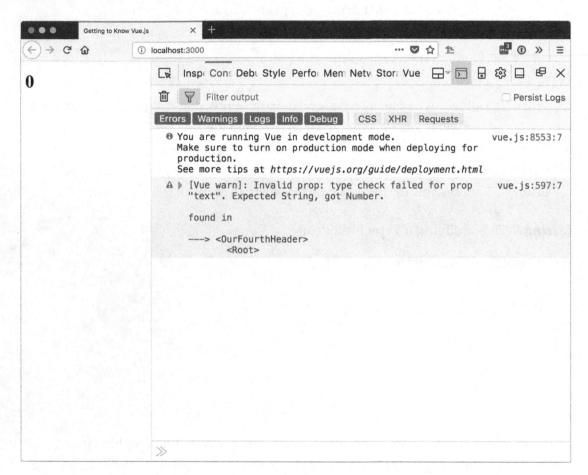

Figure 8-4. *Console error for binding the wrong value type to a prop*

To use the other options with a prop, we have to change it so that instead of a type, we specify an object as its value. We then can use the property names of this object to specify the type, default value, required or not, and the validator.

Listing 8-8 shows our text prop with a type of String, a default of App Header 5, required set to false, and a validator that checks in the text for the word app.

Listing 8-8. Specifying a props type, default, required, and validator

```
Vue.component('OurFifthHeader', {
  props: {
    text: {
      type: String,
      default: 'App Header 5',
      required: false,
      validator: function(value) {
        return value.toLowerCase().indexOf('app') > -1;
      }
    }
  },
  template: `
    <h1>{{text}}</h1>
  `
});
```

Now we can use our component with or without specifying the text prop, as shown in Listing 8-9. We also will get an error in the console if the text does not contain the word app.

Listing 8-9. Using the Default Value for the text Prop and Binding to the text Prop

```
<OurFifthHeader />
<OurFifthHeader v-bind:text="appLabel"/>
```

Viewing this in the browser results in two different headers, as shown in Figure 8-5.

Figure 8-5. *Using the default text prop value or assigning a value from the parent component*

Events

With props we can send data from a parent component to a child component. But how do we send data to the parent component from the child?

With events!

Using events, we can "listen" on the element's declaration in the parent to determine when a change occurs and react to it. To send the event, we use the $emit method from the child component. It takes two values: the name of the event and a value to pass. To receive the event, we use v-on:event-name.

In Listing 8-10, we have a custom component named `SearchBox` that emits the input event when the Enter or Escape key is pressed. It passes the target value of the keypress event so that the parent component can react to the value entered in the input box.

Listing 8-10. Emitting an Event with a Value

```
Vue.component('SearchBox', {
  template: `
    <div>
      <label>Search:</label>
      <input type="text"
        v-on:keyup.enter.esc="$emit('input', $event.target.value)" />
    </div>
  `
});
```

In the parent component, we will use `v-on:input` to assign a handler for when the event is fired.

Listing 8-11 shows our parent component using the `SearchBox` custom component and adding the event handler for an `input` event.

Listing 8-11. Listening for an Event in the Parent Component

```
<SearchBox v-on:input="search" />
```

Figure 8-6 shows the `SearchBox` in use.

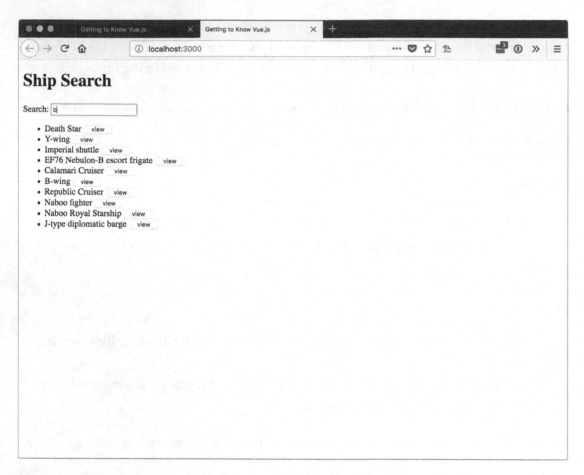

Figure 8-6. *Using events from components in action*

Using an input event might not seem that impressive since it is a native event in HTML, but what if we want to have more specific events so we can fine-tune things?

Custom events is the answer!

Just like the input event, we can create a new custom event by specifying the name of our custom event when we use $emit. In Listing 8-12, we have a custom component that is used to list a ship called ShipListItem. When its button is clicked, it emits a ship-selected event.

Listing 8-12. Emitting a Custom Event

```
Vue.component('ShipListItem', {
  props: {
    ship: {
      type: Object
    }
  },
  template: `
    <li>
      {{ship.name}} <button v-on:click="$emit('ship-selected',
      ship.url)">view</button>
    </li>
  `
});
```

On the parent component, we listen for this event with `v-on:ship-selected`. In Listing 8-13 we can see how, when the `ship-selected` event is emitted, the parent component uses a method called `viewShip` to handle the event.

Listing 8-13. Handling Custom Events

```
<ShipListItem
  v-for="ship in ships"
  v-bind:key="ship.url"
  v-bind:ship="ship"
  v-on:ship-selected="viewShip" />
```

Figure 8-7 shows the results of our custom event being fired after the view button when the Imperial shuttle is selected.

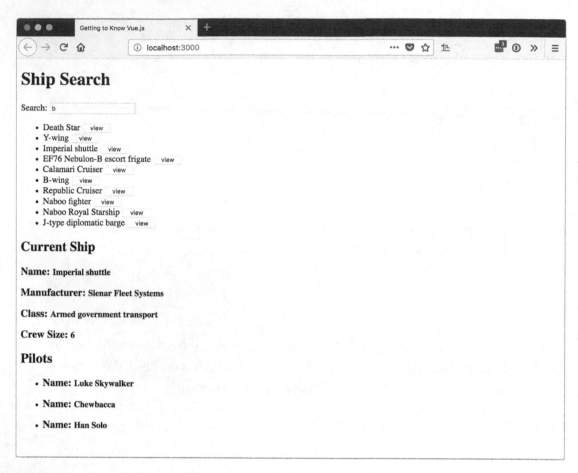

Figure 8-7. *Custom event in action*

Slots

So far, we haven't made a component that can wrap other content, but it's possible. To allow our components to wrap other content, we need to declare a `<slot>` in our component. Listing 8-14 shows the `CurrentShip` component with a `<slot></slot>` to display content.

Listing 8-14. Component with a Slot

```
Vue.component('CurrentShip', {
  computed: {
    ship: function() {
      return this.$store.state.ship;
    }
```

```
  },
  template: `
    <div v-show="ship.name">
      <h2>Current Ship</h2>

      <ShipStat label="Name" v-bind:value="ship.name" />
      <ShipStat label="Manufacturer" v-bind:value="ship.manufacturer" />
      <ShipStat label="Class" v-bind:value="ship.starship_class" />
      <ShipStat label="Crew Size" v-bind:value="ship.crew" />

      <slot></slot>
    </div>
  `
});
```

To display content in the `<slot>`, we wrap the content with the beginning and ending tags of our custom element. In Listing 8-15, we wrap the `PilotList` custom element inside the `CurrentShip` custom element.

Listing 8-15. Wrapping Content with a Custom Element

```
<CurrentShip>
  <PilotList />
</CurrentShip>
```

Registration

The components we have made up until now have been registered with Vue using `Vue.component`. This makes them all global components, available for all Vue instances created after they are registered. This is great for a simple demonstration, but if you are using a tool like Webpack, it might lead to code being bundled and sent to users that isn't needed.

Note   Webpack is a JavaScript module bundler. For more information about Webpack, visit `https://webpack.js.org/`.

To prevent unnecessary code bundling, we can use local registration. To use local registration, we define our component as an object, as shown in Listing 8-16.

Listing 8-16. Define a Custom Component for Local Registration

```
var AppHeader = {
  props: {
    text: {
      type: String,
      default: 'App Header'
    }
  },
  template: `
    <h1>{{text}}</h1>
  `
};
```

Note   Order matters. If you have a component that requires a component as a dependency, be sure to define the dependency first.

To use this `AppHeader` component, we need to register it with the instance of Vue we plan on using it with in the component's property. Listing 8-17 shows how to register our `AppHeader` in a Vue app.

Listing 8-17. Registering a Component Locally

```
var app = new Vue({
  el: '#app',
  components: {
    AppHeader: AppHeader
  },
  data: {
    appLabel: 'Ship Search'
  },
```

```
template: `
    <div>

        <AppHeader />

    </div>
    `

});
```

Summary

In this chapter, we learned all about components, including creating them, defining the data as a function, defining and passing props, emitting and handling events, using slots, and understanding the difference between global and local registration.

CHAPTER 9

Reusable Code

Components are great for reusing an entire custom element, but we can't use just a portion of the component. To share functionality among multiple components, we have to use *mixins*. Custom directives will allow us to build out functionality that we can apply to standard HTML components and custom Vue.js components. The `render` function will give us more control over how our template is built, giving us the ability to use logic in JavaScript to build our templates.

Mixins

Mixins allow us to create "base" components with common functionality that we want to share with multiple components. This can be useful for implementing a standard method that is shared, ensuring an event or action is taken during a lifecycle event, or setting default values for the data to help other components.

Creating Mixins

To create a mixin, we need to declare an options object that has implementations for the options we want to share. So, if we are going to share data, our mixin will implement a data property. This goes for the rest of the options that we want to share.

In Listing 9-1, we create a simple mixin that contains a data property of `text` set to default, a lifecycle hook to call its log method when created, a log method, and a template.

Listing 9-1. A Simple Mixin

```
var baseMixin = {
  data: function() {
    return { text: 'default' };
  },
```

© Brett Nelson 2018
B. Nelson, *Getting to Know Vue.js*, https://doi.org/10.1007/978-1-4842-3781-6_9

```
created: function() {
    this.log(`My text when Created: ${this.text}`);
},
methods: {
    log: function(...params) {
        console.log(...params);
    }
},
template: `
<div>
    <h1>{{text}}</h1>
</div>
`
};
```

It almost looks like we are defining a Vue app or component with our mixin and in a way we are, but not the entire intended app just the portions to share.

Using Mixins

With our mixin defined, we will need to register it for use with our component. We register our mixin with the component by providing an option property named `mixin` that has an array as the value with our mixins in the array. Listing 9-2 shows using the mixin from Listing 9-1.

Listing 9-2. Using a Mixin

```
var componentOne = {
    mixins: [baseMixin]
};
```

If we use `componentOne` in an app, it will show our `<h1>` with the word `default`, as shown in Figure 9-1.

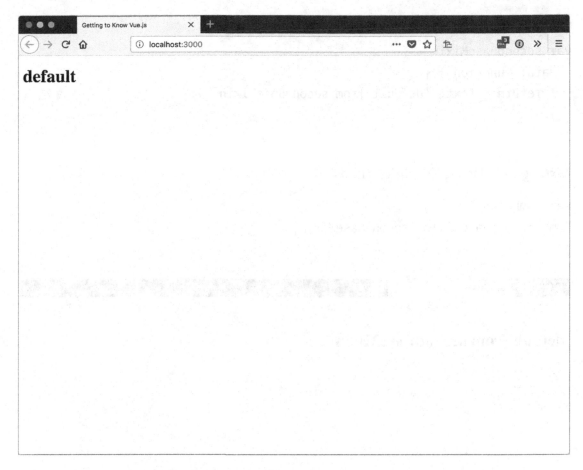

Figure 9-1. Using our baseMixin with a component

Using Multiple Mixins

You're probably thinking, "that's great and all, but what if I want to share feature set A with one set of components and feature set B with a second set of components with little overlap?" Well, the answer is to use multiple mixins.

We can use multiple mixins with the same component. By default, they will be applied in the order they are listed in the array. So element 0 is applied first, element 1 is applied second and might change some of the options from the first mixin, and so forth.

Listing 9-3 has a second mixin that sets the value of our data's `text` property. We then use this is Listing 9-4 to create `componentTwo` with two mixins. When we look at it in the browser, as shown in Figure 9-2, we see that the value of `text` is provided by `secondBaseMixin`, but nothing else has changed.

Listing 9-3. Second Mixin

```
var secondBaseMixin = {
  data: function() {
    return { text: 'default from secondBaseMixin' };
  }
};
```

Listing 9-4. Using Multiple Mixins

```
var componentTwo = {
  mixins: [baseMixin, secondBaseMixin]
};
```

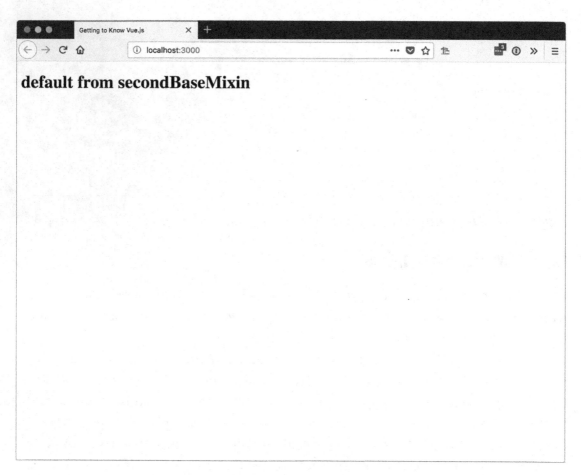

Figure 9-2. *The results of using multiple mixins*

Custom Directives

We have been using out-of-the-box directives as soon as we used our first v-if, v-show, or v-model. Custom directives allow us to apply DOM changes to plain HTML elements. similar to the directives that came with Vue.

Creating a Directive

To create a custom directive, we register it with Vue. To register it, we call Vue.directive before our Vue instance is created so that it will be available for use when our app is running.

The first parameter we will pass Vue.directive is the name of our directive. This name, prefixed with v-, is what we will use in the HTML to apply the directive to an element. The second parameter will be an object with properties to define the action to take during one or more of the following hooks:

- bind: This is called once when the directive is bound to the element.

- inserted: This is called when the element is inserted into the parent node.

- update: This is called after the element has been updated but the child elements may not have been updated yet.

- componentUpdated: This is called after the element and the child elements have been updated.

- unbind: This is called when the directive is removed.

Note   It is also possible to pass in a function instead of an object as the second parameter. This function will be called for the bind and update hooks.

The hooks will be defined as a function with access to the following parameters:

- el: This is the element the directive is bound to, thereby allowing us to change its properties.

- binding: This is an object that exposes the following values through its properties.

- name: The name of the directive minus the v-.

- value: If a value or object is passed to the directive, this is where it can be accessed.

- oldValue: This is only available with update and componentUpdated and contains the previous value.

- expression: This is the expression used in the binding as a string.

- arg: This would be the arguments passed to the directive. An example of an argument is click in the name of the event used with v-on in v-on:click="".

- modifiers: These are objects containing any modifiers. An example of a modifier is .once in the event modifiers used with v-on in v-on:click.once="".

- vnode: This is the virtual node created by Vue.

- oldVnode: This is only available with update and componentUpdated and contains the previous vnode.

With that in mind, we will create a sample directive that floats the element it is applied to using the inserted hook. Listing 9-5 has a directive called floatRight that sets the element's style.float to right.

Listing 9-5. Creating a Sample Directive

```
Vue.directive('floatRight', {
  inserted: function(el) {
    el.style.float = 'right';
  }
});
```

Using the Directive

To use our directive, we will add `v-float-right` or `v-floatRight` as an attribute to an element. In Listing 9-6, we apply it to two `<span>`s.

Listing 9-6. Using Our Custom Directive

```
var app = new Vue({
  el: '#app',
  template: `
    <div>
      <h1>Floating Directive</h1>
      <span v-float-right>
        Floated Right
      </span>
        <span v-floatRight>
        Floated Right too
      </span>

    </div>
    `
});
```

Since this is the entire app we currently have, you can see that we don't need to add the directive to the app since it was registered with Vue before the app was created. In Figure 9-3, you can see that our spans have been floated to the right.

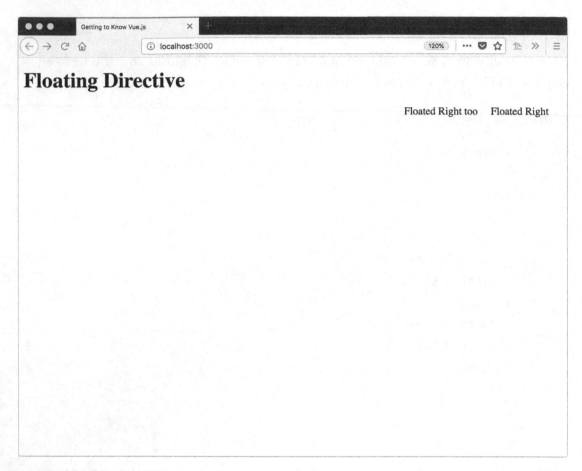

Figure 9-3. *Our custom directive in action*

Passing a Value

Since we can now float an element, we may decide it would be a good idea to give it some space away from the right side of the screen. Since we don't know how much space each situation will call for, we can pass a number to our directive as a value. In Listing 9-7, we pass 200 as a value to our custom component.

Listing 9-7. Passing a Value to a Custom Component

```
var app = new Vue({
  el: '#app',
  template: `
      <div>
```

```
      <h1>Floating Directive</h1>
      <span v-float-right="200">
        Floated Right
      </span>
    </div>
    `
});
```

To use this value, we need to make some changes to our directive. First, we need to access the binding parameter, then we check if the value is set, and if it is set, we set the value of `el.style.marginRight` to that many pixels. Listing 9-8 shows the update.

Listing 9-8. Using a Passed Value in a Custom Directive

```
Vue.directive('floatRight', {
  inserted: function(el, binding) {
    el.style.float = 'right';
    if (binding.value) {
      el.style.marginRight = `${binding.value}px`;
    }
  }
});
```

These changes will result in our floated span being a little bit away from the right edge of the screen, as shown in Figure 9-4.

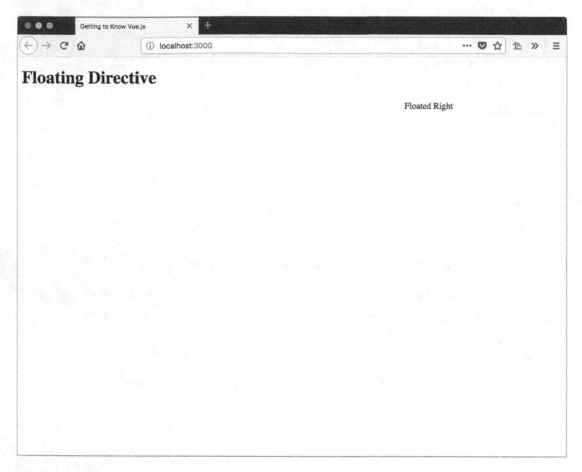

Figure 9-4. *Using passed values in a custom directive*

Passing an Object as a Value

We can also pass an object instead of a single value. In Listing 9-9, we pass an inline object literal in the first float, and then we pass an object bound to the Vue instance.

Listing 9-9. Passing Objects as Values to a Custom Directive

```
var app = new Vue({
  el: '#app',
  data: {
    floatLeft: { direction: 'left', offset: 40 }
  },
  template: `
```

```
    <div>
      <h1>Floating Directive</h1>
      <span v-float="{direction:'right', offset : 250}">
        First Floated Right
      </span>
      <span v-float="floatLeft">
        Second Floated Left
      </span>
    </div>
    `

});
```

To use the objects we are passing, we have to update our custom directive again. In Listing 9-10, we assign the value of direction to the el.style.float and then we check if there is an offset. If there is one, we use it to set the margin again.

Listing 9-10. Using Objects as Passed Values in a Custom Directive

```
Vue.directive('float', {
  inserted: function(el, binding) {
    el.style.float = binding.value.direction;
    if (binding.value.offset) {
      if (binding.value.direction === 'right') {
        el.style.marginRight = `${binding.value.offset}px`;
      } else {
        el.style.marginLeft = `${binding.value.offset}px`;
      }
    }
  }
});
```

This will allow us to use the same directive for floating both ways. We can see the results in Figure 9-5.

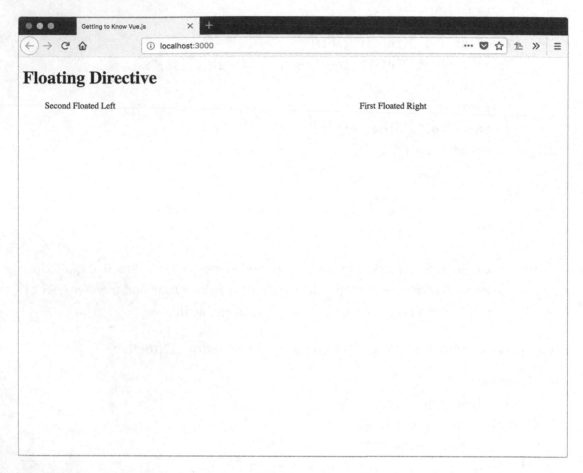

Figure 9-5. *Using objects to pass values to custom directives*

Using Modifiers

We can also use modifiers to change the behavior of our custom directive. In Listing 9-11, we use modifiers to specify the direction of the float.

Listing 9-11. Using a Modifier with Custom Directives

```
var app = new Vue({
  el: '#app',
  data: {
    floatLeft: 40
  },
```

```
template: `
    <div>
        <h1>Floating Directive</h1>
        <span v-float.right="250">
            First Floated Right
        </span>
        <span v-float.left="floatLeft">
            Second Floated Left
        </span>
    </div>
    `

});
```

In Listing 9-12, we have the implementation of custom directive, which checks if the modifier contains the value right and assigns float and margins accordingly.

Listing 9-12. Using Modifiers in a Custom Directive

```
Vue.directive('float', {
  inserted: function(el, binding) {
    if (binding.modifiers.right) {
      el.style.float = 'right';
    } else {
      el.style.float = 'left';
    }
    if (binding.value) {
      if (binding.modifiers.right) {
        el.style.marginRight = `${binding.value}px`;
      } else {
        el.style.marginLeft = `${binding.value}px`;
      }
    }
  }
});
```

The results of these changes can be seen in Figure 9-6.

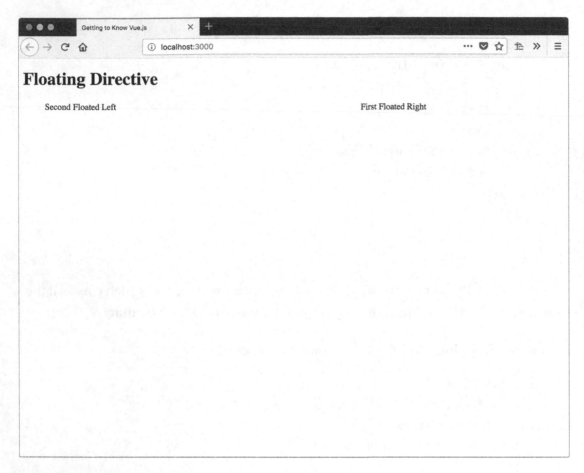

Figure 9-6. Using modifiers with a custom directive

Render Function

The render function of a Vue component gives us the full power of JavaScript to build our templates. This makes it easier to perform more concise logic than would be possible in an HTML template.

Render versus Template

We are going to look at creating a component that has three props: content, element, and background. The content will be a string that we use as the body of the component. The element will be the tag of the HTML element we want to create: h1, h2, or p. And the background will be the color we want the background of the component to be.

In Listing 9-13, we see one version of the component, templateSample. We will have to wrap everything in a <span> and use v-if to select our proper element. In Listing 9-14, we see the second component, renderSample. We will use the render function to build our component based on the properties.

Listing 9-13. Component Using Template Syntax to Select an Element Type

```
let templateSample = {
  props: {
    content: String,
    element: String,
    background: String
  },
  template: `
  <span>
    <h1 v-if="element == 'h1'"
        v-bind:style="{backgroundColor: background}">
          {{this.content}}
    </h1>
    <h2 v-else-if="element == 'h2'"
        v-bind:style="{backgroundColor: background}">
          {{this.content}}
    </h2>
    <p v-else-if="element == 'p'"
       v-bind:style="{backgroundColor: background}">
         {{this.content}}
    </p>
  </span>
  `
};
```

Listing 9-14. Component Using the render Function to Select an Element Type

```
let renderSample = {
  render: function(createElement) {
    return createElement(
      this.element,
```

```
    { style: { backgroundColor: this.background } },
      this.content
    );
  },
  props: {
    content: String,
    element: String,
    background: String
  }
};
```

In Listing 9-15, we can see our app that can use both components in the same manner.

Listing 9-15. Using the Sample Components

```
var app = new Vue({
  el: '#app',
  components: { renderSample, templateSample },
  template: `
      <div>
        <h1>Template Render</h1>
        <div>
        <templateSample
            content="Render Me!"
            element="h2"
            background="red"
        />
        <templateSample
            content="Render Me Too!"
            element="h1"
            background="lightblue"
        />
        <templateSample
            content="Hide Me!"
```

```
            element="p"
            background="black"
        />
    </div>

    <h1>Sample Render</h1>
    <div>
    <renderSample
        content="Render Me!"
        element="h2"
        background="red"
    />
    <renderSample
        content="Render Me Too!"
        element="h1"
        background="lightblue"
    />
    <renderSample
        content="Hide Me!"
        element="p"
        background="black"
    />
    </div>
    </div>
    `

});
```

Since both components use the same props, the results of using the same values should be very similar. The main difference will be the templateSample, which has a span wrapping the content so that the template has a single root element.

In Figure 9-7, we can see that the HTML created by our templateSample does have the extra <span> elements.

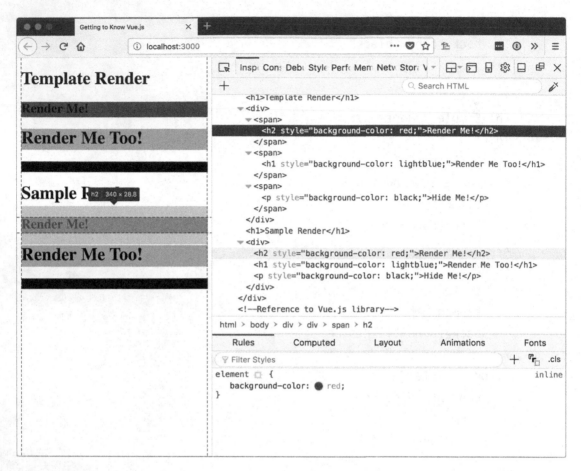

Figure 9-7. *Comparing the results of the templateSample and renderSample components*

In these sample components, you can see that using the `render` function could save a lot of duplicate markup and accomplish the same tasks as with the HTML template.

createElement

The `render` function of a component gets passed one property, the `createElement` method. The `createElement` method can be used to create virtual nodes, or `vnodes` for short. Vue uses the `vnodes` to construct a "virtual DOM" out of all the components of an app.

Parameter One

To create elements with `createElement` we can pass it up to three parameters. The first parameter can be the HTML tag of the element to be created, the component options that create a Vue component, or a function that returns one of the previous results.

In Listing 9-16, we use `createElement` and provide it with a p to generate a `<p>` tag. The second parameter in this example is the default slot, so any child elements or text will be wrapped by our element.

Listing 9-16. Using the render Function to Create a p Element

```
let tagElement = {
  render: function(createElement) {
    return createElement('p', this.$slots.default);
  }
};
```

In Listing 9-17, we use `createElement` with a Vue `options` object to create an element that has a prop to pass in the content. The content is then passed to the data object for the `options` object that is used to render the component.

Listing 9-17. Using the render Function to Create an Element with a Vue Options Object

```
let optionsElement = {
  props: {
    content: String
  },
  render: function(createElement) {
    let data = { contentToRender: this.content };
    return createElement({
      data: function() {
        return data;
      },
      template: '<p>{{contentToRender}}</p>'
    });
  }
};
```

In Listing 9-18, we can see that both components are used in a similar manner and in Figure 9-8 we see that the results are the same.

Listing 9-18. Using a Component Created from a Tag and a Component Created from an Options Object

```
var app = new Vue({
  el: '#app',
  components: { tagElement, optionsElement },
  template: `
    <div>
      <h1>Template Render</h1>
      <div>
      <tagElement>Paragraph 1</tagElement>
      <optionsElement content="Paragraph 2"></optionsElement>
      </div>
    </div>
    `
});
```

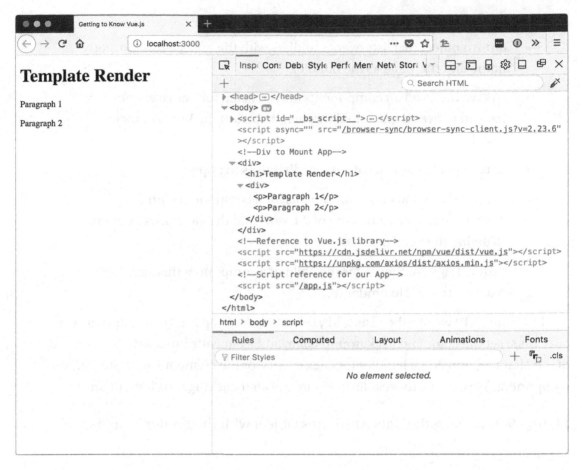

Figure 9-8. *Rendering tagElement and the optionsElement in the browser*

Parameter Two

The second parameter represents the data attributes of the element to be created and is optional. Properties that can be set with this object are as follows:

- `class:` Uses the same syntax as when using `v-bind:class` in a template.

- `style:` Uses the same syntax as when using `v-bind:style` in a template.

- `attrs:` An object that contains property names of attributes to bind with the values provided for each property.

- `props:` Props to bind on the component.

- domProps: DOM properties to bind on the element.

- on: An object that lists event handlers with the event as the property name and the value as the handler.

- nativeOn: Used on components only to listen for native events instead of events generated through the use of the Vue instance $emit.

- directives: An array of custom directives to apply.

- scopedSlots: An object of the slots for a component with the property names as the name of the slots and the value as a function to define the content.

- slot: If this component is the child of a component this specifies the name of the slot to render in.

In Listing 9-19 we use the class, style, attrs, domProps, and on to add the class ourClass, set the color and background color, add a data attribute, set the inner text of the element, and add a handler for click events for the element we create with our component. We can see the results in Figure 9-9 after clicking the element once.

Listing 9-19. Using the Data Attributes Object with the render Function

```
let dataElement = {
  methods: {
    handleClick: function() {
      console.log('data element clicked');
    }
  },
  render: function(createElement) {
    return createElement('p', {
      class: {
        ourClass: true
      },
      style: {
        color: '#34495E',
        backgroundColor: '#41B883'
      },
```

```
    attrs: {
      'data-secret': "shh don't tell"
    },
    domProps: {
      innerText: 'Getting To Know Vue.js'
    },
    on: {
      click: this.handleClick
    }
  });
  }
};
```

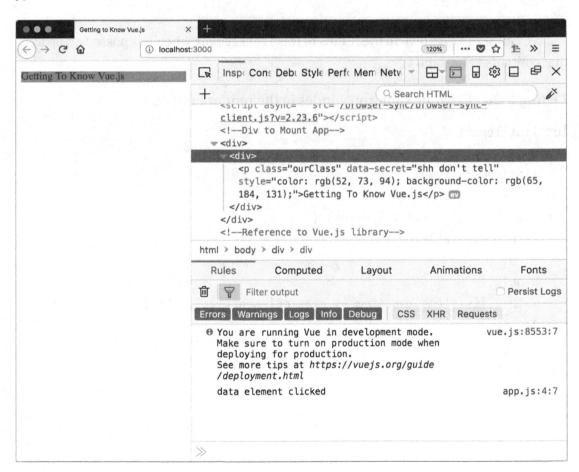

Figure 9-9. *Rendering a component that uses the data attributes object with the render function*

Parameter Three

The third parameter represents any children vnodes and is optional. It can be a string only if the child element is text or an array of vnodes.

In Listing 9-20, we create a component that accepts a prop called `listItems`, which is an array. In the `render` function, we use the map function of the array to go through the items and create new elements for each item in the array. This effectively returns a new array of vnodes as the third parameter.

Note   The `null` in the second parameter in Listing 9-20 is not required. I used it in this example so that the position would be maintained when referencing the third parameter.

We can see in Figure 9-10 the results of this `listElement` when it is passed an array that contains 1, Two, and C.

Listing 9-20. Creating Children vnodes in the render Function

```
let listElement = {
  props: {
    listItems: Array
  },
  render: function(createElement) {
    return createElement(
      'ul',
      null,
      this.listItems.map(item => createElement('li', item))
    );
  }
};
```

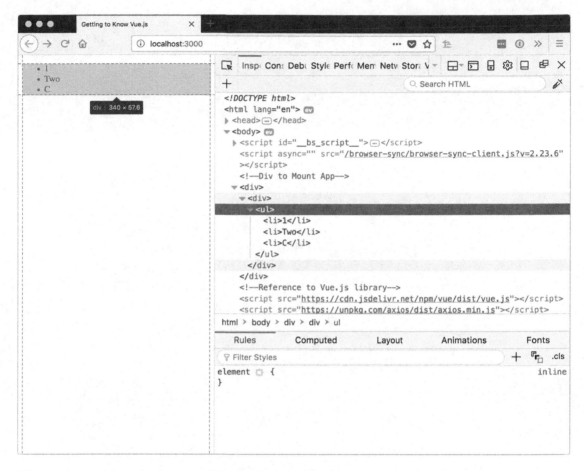

Figure 9-10. *Rendering our listElement in the browser*

Summary

In this chapter, we learned how to use mixins to create functionality that can be shared with components that are based on the mixin. We also learned about creating custom directives, which allow us to add functionality to standard HTML elements and to our own components. We finished by learning how we can write less code using the `render` function than if we build the template with markup.

CHAPTER 10

Custom Functionality

Plugins offer a way to extend the global functionality of Vue by creating default behavior, adding global components, or generally creating values throughout your Vue app. Filters allow us to create reusable text transformation that we can apply to our templates. Let's take a look at how to create and use these features in Vue.

Plugins

Plugins allow us to expand Vue to meet our needs in a manner that we can share with other Vue apps without sharing our entire app.

Creating a Plugin

To create a plugin, make a JavaScript object that exposes an `install` function. The `install` function accepts two parameters: Vue and `options`. The Vue parameter is the global Vue that will be used to create our app.

We can add to the prototype of Vue and all instances created after `install` is called and they will gain access to the plugin. In Listing 10-1, we create a plugin that adds an object to Vue's prototype named `$_customPlugin`.

Note   It is recommended that you prefix any private properties with $_ and add the name of the plugin to scope the properties. This is to prevent conflicts with anything that developers using your plugins use.

B. Nelson, *Getting to Know Vue.js*, https://doi.org/10.1007/978-1-4842-3781-6_10

Listing 10-1. Creating a Small Plugin

```
let customPlugin = {
  install: function(Vue, options) {
    Vue.prototype.$_customPlugin = {
      name: 'Getting to Know Vue.js'
    };
  }
};
```

Using a Plugin

Before we can use our plugin, we have to install it with Vue. To install our plugin, we call Vue.use(customPlugin) before we create our app. In Listing 10-2, we install our plugin before creating our Vue app. We can also see how we have access to the $_customPlugin of this in our app. This results in the browser displaying the results in Figure 10-1.

Listing 10-2. Installing a Plugin and Accessing its Properties

```
Vue.use(customPlugin);

var app = new Vue({
  el: '#app',
  template: `
      <div>
        <h1>
          {{this.$_customPlugin.name}}
        </h1>
      </div>
      `
});
```

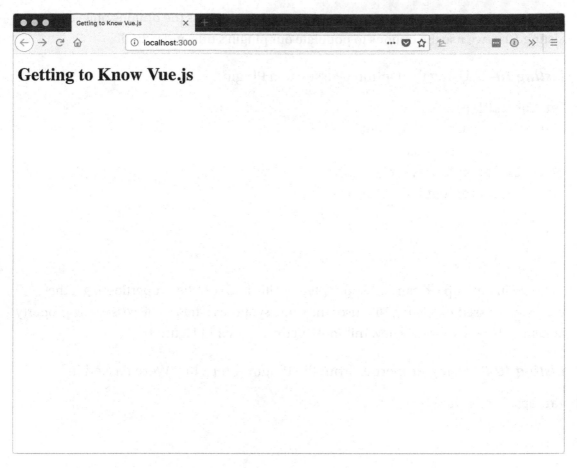

Figure 10-1. *Our first plugin in action*

Using Options

We can also pass in options when installing our plugin. To pass in options, we include a second parameter when calling Vue.use, an option object. We can see this in Listing 10-3, where we use an options object that has two properties when calling Vue.use.

Listing 10-3. Passing an Options Object to a Plugin

```
Vue.use(customPlugin, {
  title: 'Getting to Know Vue.js',
  subTitle: 'Now with Options'
});
```

In our plugin, we can use the second parameter to access the options object. In Listing 10-4, we use the options to populate our plugin's title and subtitle.

Listing 10-4. Using the Options Passed to a Plugin

```
let customPlugin = {
  install: function(Vue, options) {
    Vue.prototype.$_customPlugin = {
      title: options.title,
      subtitle: options.subtitle
    };
  }
};
```

Now in our app we can access our plugins title and subtitle properties to get the values we passed in. Listing 10-5 uses the same syntax as when we accessed the property in Listing 10-2. We can see how this looks in the browser in Figure 10-2.

Listing 10-5. Using Properties from the Plugin After They Were Passed In

```
var app = new Vue({
  el: '#app',
  template: `
      <div>
        <h1>
          {{this.$_customPlugin.title}}
          <small>
            {{this.$_customPlugin.subtitle }}
          </small>
        </h1>
      </div>
      `
});
```

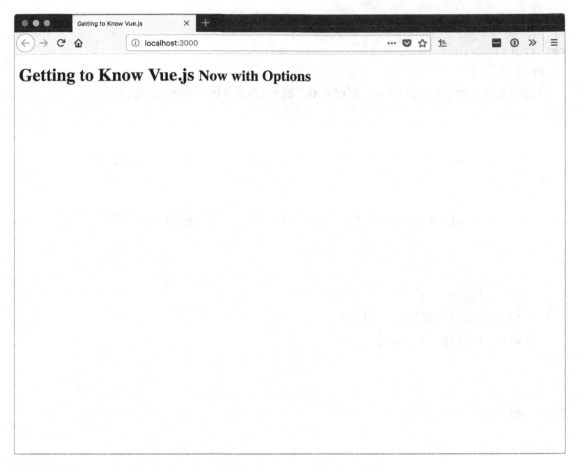

Figure 10-2. *Using our plugin with options*

Registering a Global Mixin with a Plugin

We can also add functionality to all instances of Vue created after we register our plugin by registering a global mixin. In Listing 10-6, we create a plugin that registers a global mixin to add a console log statement with the time when a Vue instance is created, mounted, and updated. We can see this output in our developer console in Figure 10-3.

Listing 10-6. Using a Plugin to Register a Global Mixin

```
var logLifecyle = {
  created() {
    console.log(`Created at ${new Date().toLocaleTimeString()}`);
  },
  mounted() {
    console.log(`Mounted at ${new Date().toLocaleTimeString()}`);
  },
  updated() {
    console.log(`Updated at ${new Date().toLocaleTimeString()}`);
  }
};

let customPlugin = {
  install: function(Vue, options) {
    Vue.mixin(logLifecyle);
  }
};

Vue.use(customPlugin);

var app = new Vue({
  el: '#app',
  template: `
      <div>
        <h1>
         Getting to Know Vue.js
        </h1>
      </div>
      `
});
```

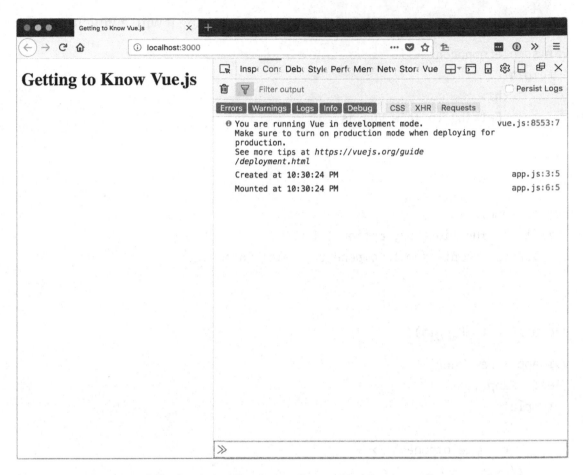

Figure 10-3. *Our global mixin that logs when a Vue instance is created and mounted*

Registering Global Components with a Plugin

We can also share components with a plugin by registering components globally.

In Listing 10-7, we create a component, register it with our plugin globally, and use it in our app. The results can be seen in Figure 10-4.

Listing 10-7. Registering a Global Component and Using it with a Plugin

```
var sampleComponent = {
  template: `
        <h1>
         Getting to Know Vue.js
        </h1>
        `
};

let customPlugin = {
  install: function(Vue, options) {
    Vue.component('sampleComponent', sampleComponent);
  }
};

Vue.use(customPlugin);

var app = new Vue({
  el: '#app',
  template: `
      <div>
        <sampleComponent />
      </div>
        `

});
```

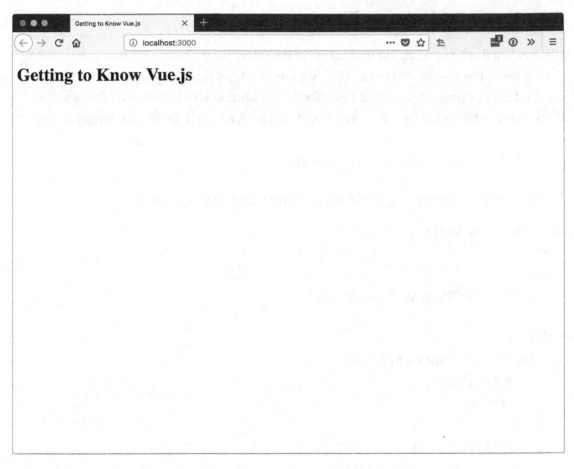

Figure 10-4. Using our global component from a plugin

Filters

Filters allow us to create reusable text transformations that can be used in our templates where we bind using the mustache syntax `{{ value }}` or when we bind a value using `v-bind:`.

Creating and Using a Filter

We create a filter as a function that takes a value, does something with that value, and then returns the results. In Listing 10-7, we create a filter that's registered with our app via the `filters` property, named `lowerCase`. The function for lowercase takes a value. If the value is false (`false`, `null`, `undefined`, `0`, `NaN`, `'`, or `""`) it returns an empty string; otherwise, we call `toString` on the value, so we know that we are dealing with text before calling `toLowerCase` and returning the results.

Listing 10-7. Creating a Filter That Converts Text to Lowercase

```
var app = new Vue({
  el: '#app',
  data: {
    title: 'Getting to Know Vue.js'
  },
  filters: {
    lowercase: function(value) {
      if (!value) {
        return ";
      }
      let text = value.toString();
      return text.toLowerCase();
    }
  },
  template: `
    <div>
      <h1>{{ title | lowercase }}</h1>

      <input
          type="text"
          v-bind:placeholder="title | lowercase" />
    </div>
    `
});
```

In Listing 10-7, we also see that to apply a filter in the mustache template binding, we use a single pipe (|) after the value in the <h1>. For the <input> we use a single pipe following the value with the v-bind: syntax. This all ends up looking like Figure 10-5 when viewed in the browser.

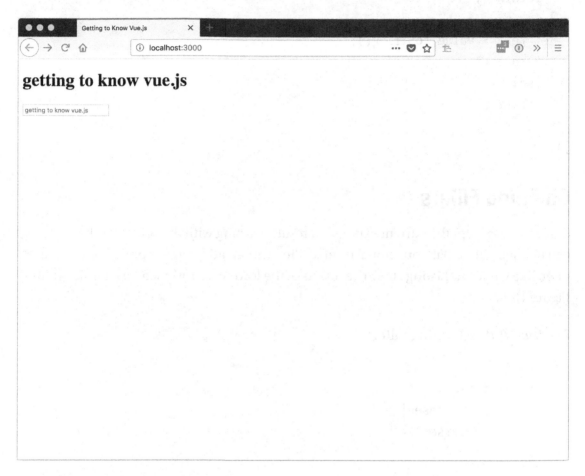

Figure 10-5. *Using our filter to transform our text to all lowercase*

Creating a Global Filter

To create a filter that is available for use in all Vue instances without defining it on each, we can register it using the global method before creating our app.

To register a filter globally, we call Vue.filter, passing in the name and the implementation as parameters. Listing 10-8 shows a global filter named reverse. Its implementation reverses the text of a string.

Listing 10-8. Registering a Global Filter

```
Vue.filter('reverse', function(value) {
  if (!value) {
    return ";
  }
  let text = value.toString();
  return text
    .split(")
    .reverse()
    .join(");
});
```

Chaining Filters

Since filters accept the current expression results starting with the original value, we can change filters. With our global reverse filter, we can add it to our previous lowercase filter, like we see in Listing 10-9. The results of the lowercase reversed text are shown in Figure 10-6.

Listing 10-9. Chaining Filters

```
<div>
  <h1>{{ title |
        lowercase |
        reverse }}</h1>

  <input
      type="text"
      v-bind:placeholder="title |
                          lowercase |
                          reverse" />
</div>
```

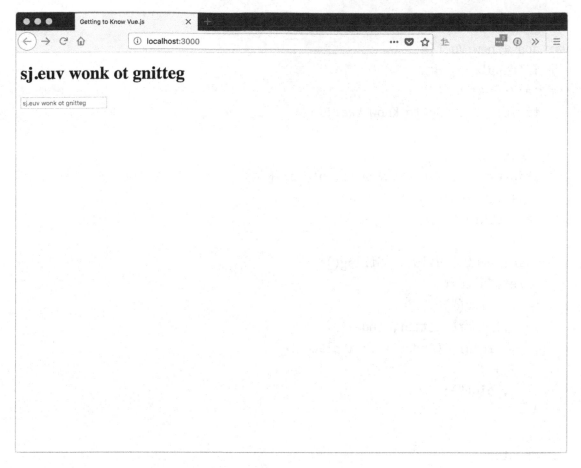

Figure 10-6. *Viewing our chained filters in a browser*

Arguments

Since filters are JavaScript functions, we can pass additional parameters to use in the filters implementation.

To pass additional arguments to the filter, we add the parameters in parentheses, separated by commas following the filter name. These parameters will be available in the filters implementation in order, following the original value that is passed to the filter.

Listing 10-10 shows a filter named `skipLetters`, which accepts a second parameter called `place`. We use `place` to skip letters. Figure 10-7 shows the results of skipping every two places for `<h1>` and every three places for `<input>`.

Listing 10-10. Passing Parameters to a Filter

```
var app = new Vue({
  el: '#app',
  data: {
    title: 'Getting to Know Vue.js'
  },
  filters: {
    skipLetters: function(value, place) {
      if (!value) {
        return ";
      }
      let text = value.toString();
      return text
        .split(")
        .filter((letter, index) => {
          return (index + 1) % place !== 0;
        })
        .join(");
    }
  },
  template: `
  <div>

    <h1><small>Original:</small> {{ title }}</h1>

    <h1><small>Skip every Two:</small> {{ title |
          skipLetters(2) }}</h1>

    <label>Skip every 4:
      <input
          type="text"
          v-bind:placeholder="title |
                            skipLetters(3)" />
    </label>
  </div>

  `
});
```

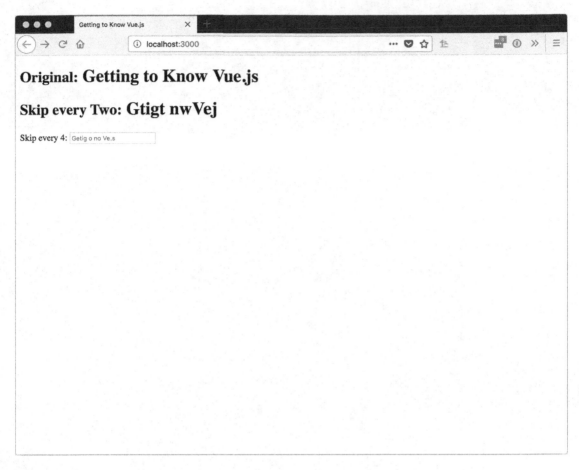

Figure 10-7. Using parameters to get different results from the same filter

Summary

In this chapter, we learned about creating a plugin to develop global functionality that can be used in more than one Vue project. We also learned about creating filters to alter the content of text when bound with mustache syntax or when using v-bind: in a template.

CHAPTER 11

Tooling

Tooling support and build tools can greatly improve the development experience in any workflow and that is as true with Vue as well. In this chapter, we will learn about single file components and the Vue command-line interface.

Single File Components

Single File Components, or SFCs, allow us to build Vue components in a single file with separate sections for the template, the JavaScript, and the styles. This allows us to take advantage of syntax highlighting and code suggestions for the language that is specified for a particular section.

SFC use the `.vue` file extension.

To use SFCs, we need a build tool in order to incorporate a build tool like Browserify or Webpack. The next main section, "Command-Line Interface," covers how to use the command-line interface to serve a Vue app that uses SFCs.

SFC Structure

The three sections of an SFC are as follows:

- Template: This section allows us to create the template for our component and get full syntax support for the markup.

- Script: This section contains our JavaScript and lets us use module syntax.

- Style: This section contains our CSS styles.

Listing 11-1 is an example of a SFC that contains the template for an `<h1>` that's used to display the `displayText` property.

© Brett Nelson 2018
B. Nelson, *Getting to Know Vue.js*, https://doi.org/10.1007/978-1-4842-3781-6_11

Listing 11-1. Example Single File Component

```
<template>
    <h1>
        Title: {{ displayText }}
    </h1>
</template>

<script>
export default {
  data() {
    return {
      displayText: 'Getting to Know Vue.js'
    };
  }
};
</script>

<style scoped>
h1 {
  color: blue;
}
</style>
```

You may have noticed the `scoped` property on the `<style>` element. By using SFC and CSS preprocessors, we will be able to scope our styles to the component. This won't prevent us from using styles that are global, but it will allow us to target specific elements in our component regardless of where it is located in the DOM tree.

Syntax Highlighting

One of the advantages of SFC is the ability of tools, like our editor, to understand the content in each section. So, the `<template>` entry is highlighted and gets suggestions like it's HTML. The `<script>` is highlighted and gets suggestions like it's JavaScript. And the `<style>` looks like a stylesheet. Figure 11-1 shows how Listing 11-1 looks in Visual Studio code.

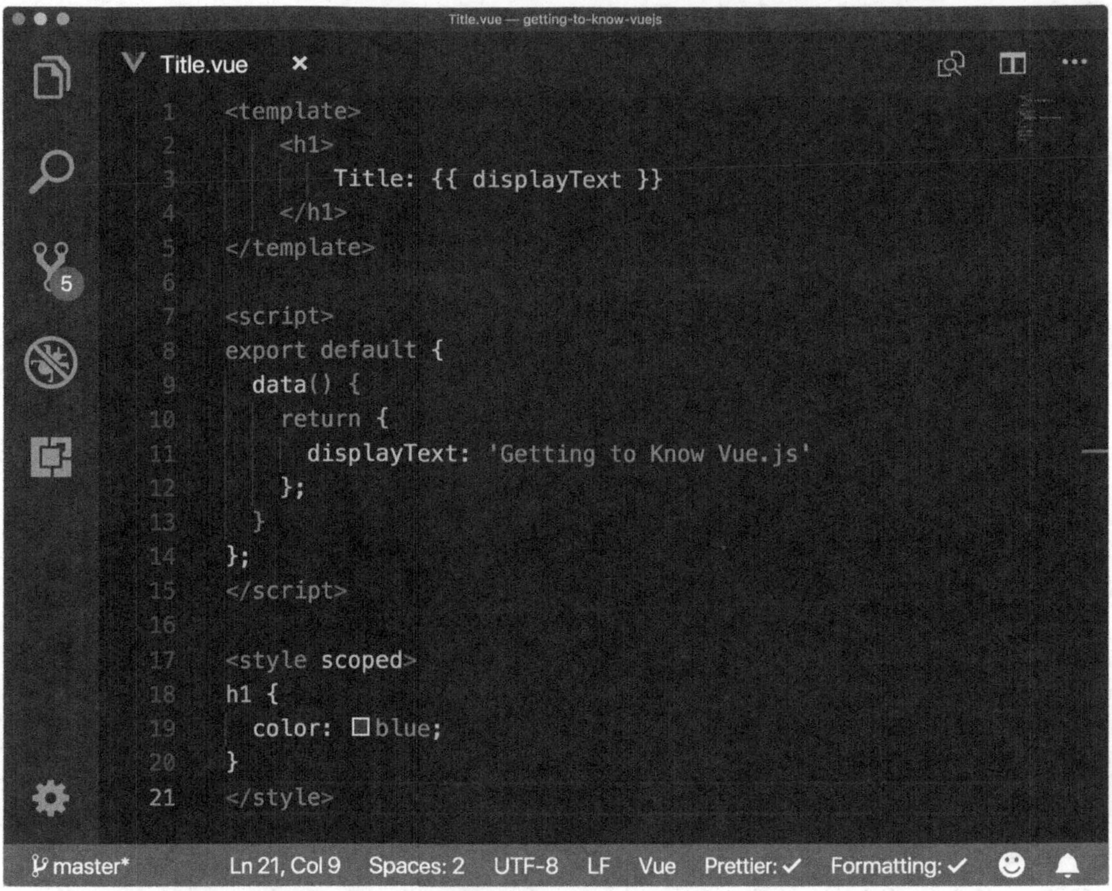

```vue
1   <template>
2     <h1>
3       Title: {{ displayText }}
4     </h1>
5   </template>
6
7   <script>
8   export default {
9     data() {
10      return {
11        displayText: 'Getting to Know Vue.js'
12      };
13    }
14  };
15  </script>
16
17  <style scoped>
18  h1 {
19    color: □blue;
20  }
21  </style>
```

Figure 11-1. *Our Vue single file component in an editor*

Since I am using Visual Studio code, `https://code.visualstudio.com/`, I am also using an extension to add Vue-related functionality called the Vue VS Code Extension Pack, which you can get at `https://marketplace.visualstudio.com/items?itemName=sdras.vue-vscode-extensionpack`.

Command-Line Interface

Now that we have an understanding of SFCs, we will take some time to figure out how to get them into a format so they can be used by a web browser. The Vue command-line interfaces, Vue CLI, allows us to use SFCs along with some other features that help with development.

With the Vue CLI, we will be able to generate projects with `vue create`, prototypes with `vue serve`, and builds for production with `vue build`.

Note   Vue CLI version 3 Release Candidate 3 was the latest release at the time of writing.

Prerequisites

To use the Vue CLI, you need some familiarity with the Node Package Manager (NPM). NPM is installed when Node.js is installed; directions can be found at `https://www.npmjs.com/get-npm`.

Once Node.js and NPM are installed, we will be able to install the Vue CLI.

Note   If you prefer Yarn, `https://yarnpkg.com`, it can also be used to install the Vue CLI.

Installing Vue CLI

To install the Vue CLI, you need to open a terminal, or command prompt if you prefer, and enter `npm install -g @vue/cli`. Once that completes, you should see something similar to Figure 11-2 on a Mac or Linux machine or something like Figure 11-3 in Windows.

```
●●●                  ▦ Example_01 — brett@Bretts-MBP — ..02/Example_01 — -zsh — 62×25
→  Example_01 git:(master) × npm install -g @vue/cli
/usr/local/bin/vue -> /usr/local/lib/node_modules/@vue/cli/bin
/vue.js

> fsevents@1.2.4 install /usr/local/lib/node_modules/@vue/cli/
node_modules/fsevents
> node install

[fsevents] Success: "/usr/local/lib/node_modules/@vue/cli/node
_modules/fsevents/lib/binding/Release/node-v57-darwin-x64/fse.
node" already installed
Pass --update-binary to reinstall or --build-from-source to re
compile

> nodemon@1.17.5 postinstall /usr/local/lib/node_modules/@vue/
cli/node_modules/nodemon
> node bin/postinstall || exit 0

+ @vue/cli@3.0.0-rc.3
added 680 packages from 471 contributors in 23.44s
→  Example_01 git:(master) × ▯
```

Figure 11-2. *Installing Vue CLI on Mac/Linux*

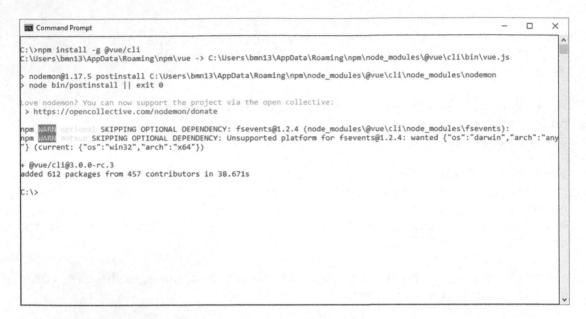

Figure 11-3. *Installing Vue CLI on Windows*

Now you should be ready to create a project.

Vue Create

With the Vue CLI installed, we can create a project from the command line by entering vue create project-name, where project-name is the name we want to give our project. This will start the process of creating our app.

For our example app, let's use the name getting-to-know-vue, as shown in Listing 11-2.

Listing 11-2. Creating a Vue App with the Vue CLI

```
vue create getting-to-know-vue
```

The first thing you might notice in Figure 11-4 is that we are given a choice on using the default project or manually choosing our options. For now, let's use the default options.

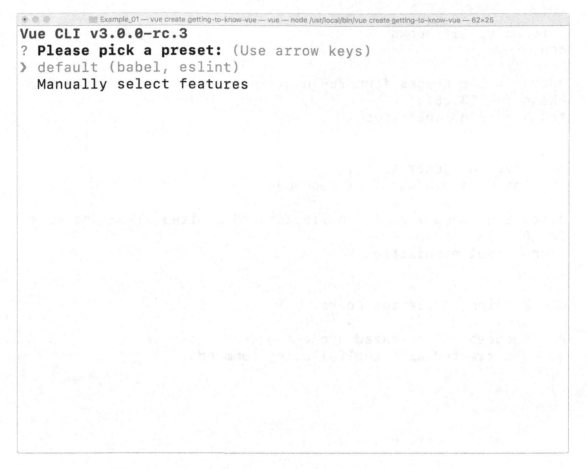

Figure 11-4. Selecting our configuration options

Once we make the selection, we should see some action in the terminal while the project is being created. It will eventually stop with something similar to Figure 11-5.

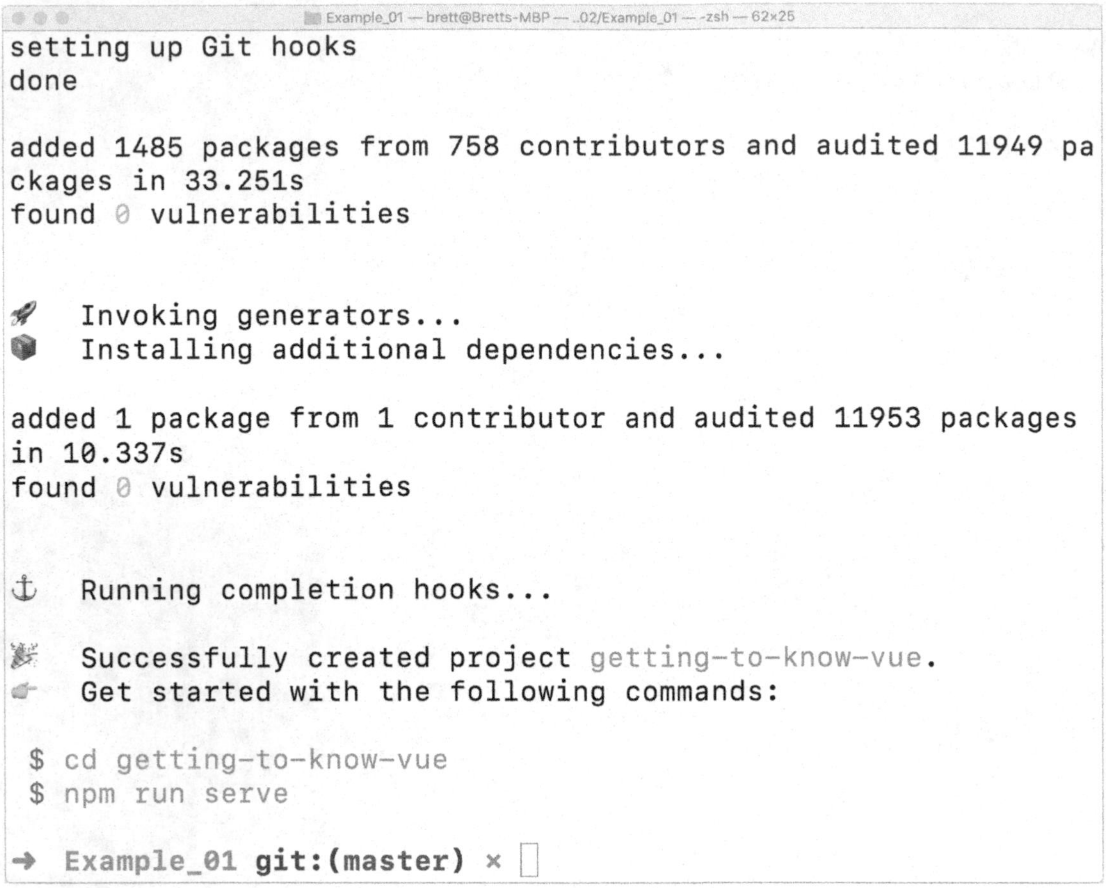

```
                  Example_01 — brett@Bretts-MBP — ..02/Example_01 — -zsh — 62×25
setting up Git hooks
done

added 1485 packages from 758 contributors and audited 11949 pa
ckages in 33.251s
found 0 vulnerabilities


🚀    Invoking generators...
📦    Installing additional dependencies...

added 1 package from 1 contributor and audited 11953 packages
in 10.337s
found 0 vulnerabilities


⚓    Running completion hooks...

🎉    Successfully created project getting-to-know-vue.
👉    Get started with the following commands:

 $ cd getting-to-know-vue
 $ npm run serve

➜  Example_01 git:(master) ✗ ▯
```

Figure 11-5. *Successfully created a Vue app with the Vue CLI*

Vue Serve

Now that the app is ready, we can follow the directions by going into the project with cd getting-to-know-vue and using the command npm run serve to see what we have to start with. The npm run serve command was created by the CLI when our project was created to use Vue-CLI-Service as a local developer server.

Running the npm run serve command from the directory created with vue create should result in the terminal looking like Figure 11-6.

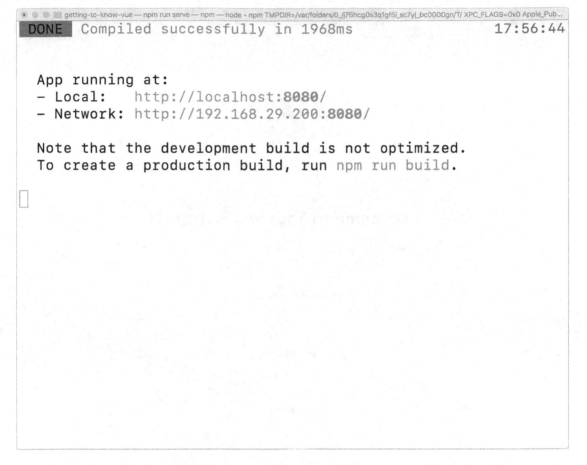

Figure 11-6. *Running the npm run serve command*

Now we can open the browser to http://localhost:8080/ or http://192.168.29.200:8080/ from a different computer on the same network to see what we have to start with.

Figure 11-7 shows the starting app in a desktop browser and Figure 11-8 shows it on a separate mobile device.

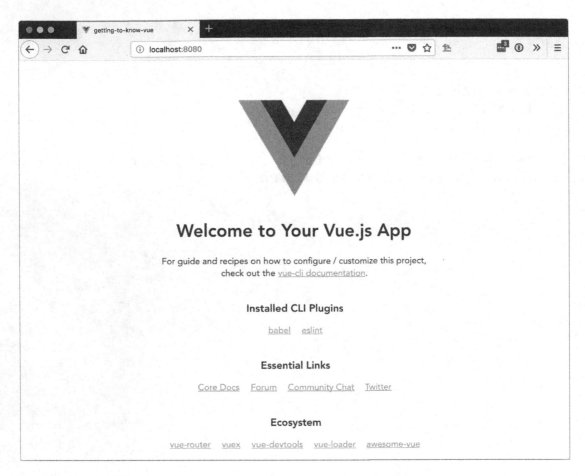

Figure 11-7. *The first look at our new Vue app on a desktop*

Figure 11-8. *The first look at our new Vue app on a mobile device*

Before we make it our own, let's see what we have to start with.

Project Structure

Figure 11-9 shows the structure created by the Vue CLI.

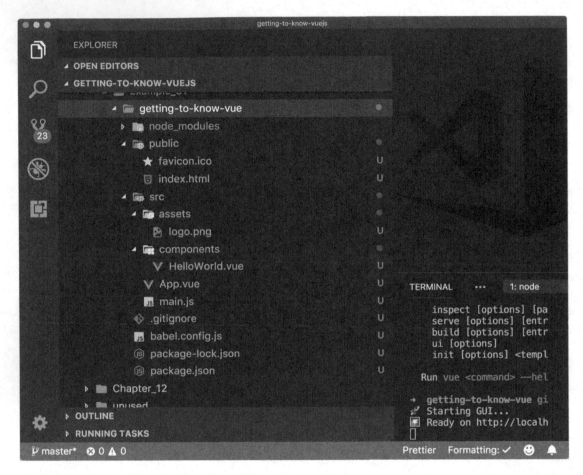

Figure 11-9. *The project structure created by the Vue CLI*

Project Root

The project root folder contains the node_modules, public, and src directories.

- node_modules contains all the dependencies downloaded from NPM when the project was created.

- public contains any items we want to expose for our app as if from the root URL, like favicon.ico and index.html.

- src contains our Vue app. We will look at this more in a moment.

Other items in the project's root folder are .gitignore, babel.config.js, package-lock.json, and package.json.

- .gitignore is used to specify what Git should not track if you are using that as a source control.

- babel.config.js is the config for Babel, https://babeljs.io/, which is a JavaScript transpiler. This makes it possible to use JavaScript features that have not yet been implemented in all browsers.

- package-lock.json is used by NPM to track the specific versions of each dependency used so that future installs will use the same versions.

- package.json is used to track our project's configurations, dependencies, and NPM scripts.

The src Folder

The src folder is where we will spend most of our time working since it's where we will keep the source of our Vue app before it is transpiled, or preprocessed, to be served to the browser. Figure 11-10 shows the expanded src directory.

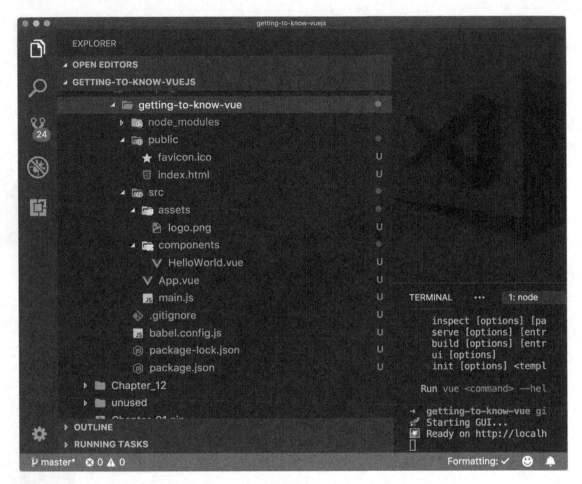

Figure 11-10. *The src directory structure*

We can see that we have a directory for `assets`, `components`, our `App.Vue`, and a `main.js` file.

- The `assets` directory contains asset references and components. The build process will provide these assets.

- The `components` folder is where we keep our components.

- `App.Vue` is the main file for our app.

- `main.js` is the starting point that mounts the app.

App.vue

The App.vue is the main container for our app. If we have anything that we want to apply to the entire app, we should do that here. Let's take a look at what we start with.

Listing 11-3 shows the App.vue we are starting with. It includes the three sections of the SFC: <template>, <script>, and <style>.

Listing 11-3. App.vue Before We Start Making Changes

```
<template>
  <div id="app">
    <img src="./assets/logo.png">
    <HelloWorld msg="Welcome to Your Vue.js App"/>
  </div>
</template>

<script>
import HelloWorld from './components/HelloWorld.vue';

export default {
  name: 'app',
  components: {
    HelloWorld
  }
};
</script>

<style>
#app {
  font-family: 'Avenir', Helvetica, Arial, sans-serif;
  -webkit-font-smoothing: antialiased;
  -moz-osx-font-smoothing: grayscale;
  text-align: center;
  color: #2c3e50;
  margin-top: 60px;
}
</style>
```

In `<template>`, we can see that it's creating a `<div>` with an `id` of app along with using the logo from the asset's directory and using the custom component `<HelloWorld>` to display a message. The logo has an URL of `./assets/logo.png` but after the app is built and served by the browser, it will be served from an URL specified by the Vue CLI build.

The `<script>` element uses the CommonJS `import` command to access the `HelloWorld` custom component before adding to the app via the Vue options object.

The `<style>` element targets the `#app` that was specified in `<template>` to apply styles with CSS.

Title.vue

The `HelloWorld` custom component is a little busy, so let's delete it and remove its import from the `App.vue`. That way, we can use the `Title.vue` SFC we looked at in Listing 11-1. Figure 11-11 shows the `Title.vue` component in the editor.

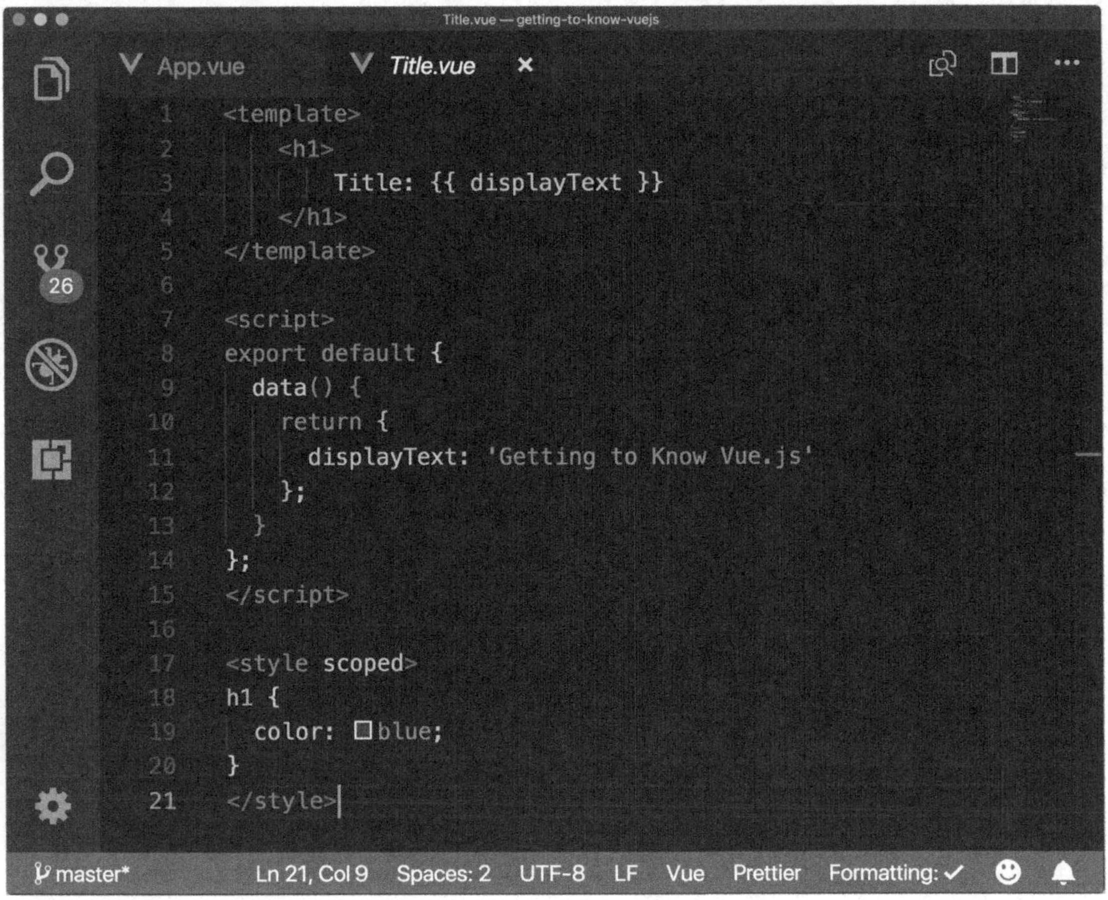

Figure 11-11. *The Title.vue component*

To use of this component, we need to import it to our App.vue with an import statement and add it to the components of the app in the <script> section. We will then have to use it in our <template> if we want it to show up, so let's add it after the logo. Listing 11-4 shows the complete App.Vue with updates.

Listing 11-4. Using Our Title.vue Custom Component in the App.vue File

```
<template>
  <div id="app">
    <img src="./assets/logo.png">
    <Title/>
  </div>
</template>

<script>
import Title from './components/Title.vue';

export default {
  name: 'app',
  components: {
    Title
  }
};
</script>

<style>
#app {
  font-family: 'Avenir', Helvetica, Arial, sans-serif;
  -webkit-font-smoothing: antialiased;
  -moz-osx-font-smoothing: grayscale;
  text-align: center;
  color: #2c3e50;
  margin-top: 60px;
}
</style>
```

Rebuild and Serve

Before you save the `App.vue` file, you might want to bring the terminal back up where you ran `vue serve`. When you save `App.vue`, the terminal should flash `Compiling...` briefly along with some updates about what step is currently being performed. Since our app is so small at this point, you may not see more than a flash of the screen updating when you press the same in your editor. Figure 11-12 shows the Compiling screen.

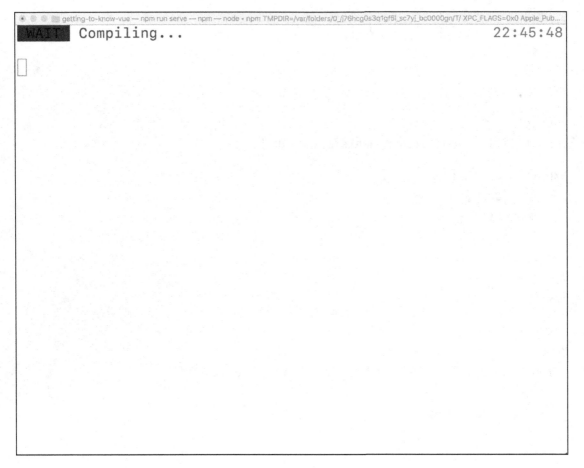

Figure 11-12. *Recompiling our app when a change occurs*

Since our app has been rebuilt, we should see it update in the browser, similar to Figure 11-13.

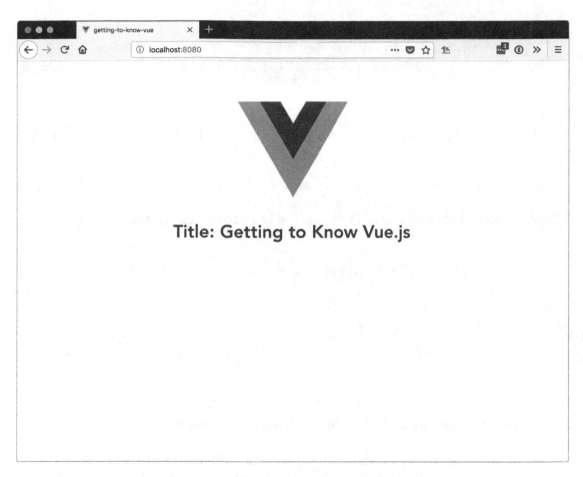

Figure 11-13. *Updating the app using the Title.vue component*

Vue Build

With all we have done so far with the Vue CLI, we have been working in dev mode. If we want to build for production, we will run the `vue build` command. To run `vue build`, we use the `npm run build` command. Once the build completes, we should get a summary of the results, similar to Figure 11-14.

```
●  ●  ●              getting-to-know-vue — brett@Bretts-MBP — ..g-to-know-vue — -zsh — 62×25
 DONE    Compiled successfully in 5339ms                    23:03:42

   File                                      Size              Gzip
ped

   dist/js/chunk-vendors.493d0141.js      74.14 kb            26.8
1 kb
   dist/js/app.df0e1095.js                 2.43 kb            1.17
 kb
   dist/css/app.f4d01213.css               0.19 kb            0.17
 kb

   Images and other types of assets omitted.

 DONE    Build complete. The dist directory is ready to be deplo
yed.

→  getting-to-know-vue git:(master) × █
```

Figure 11-14. *Summary results after building our Vue app*

In our project directory we should now have a new directory called dist. In dist we should have three directories—css, img, and js—for the app's styles, images, and JavaScript, respectively. You will also see index.html and the favicon.ico from the public directory of our src.

Now that we have our dist directory, we can put it on our public server and share our wonderful minimized app with the world.

The CLI User Interface

With Vue CLI version 3, a UI has been added, so we can do the same tasks we do from the command line using a web interface. To start the UI, enter vue ui on the command line. A web browser should open, as shown in Figure 11-15.

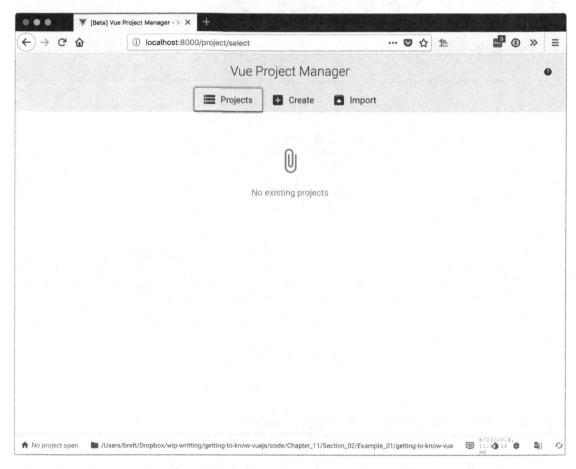

Figure 11-15. *The Vue CLI UI on first load*

Since we already have a project, we can add it using the Import menu on the top of the screen. This menu lets us browse to our project, as shown in Figure 11-16.

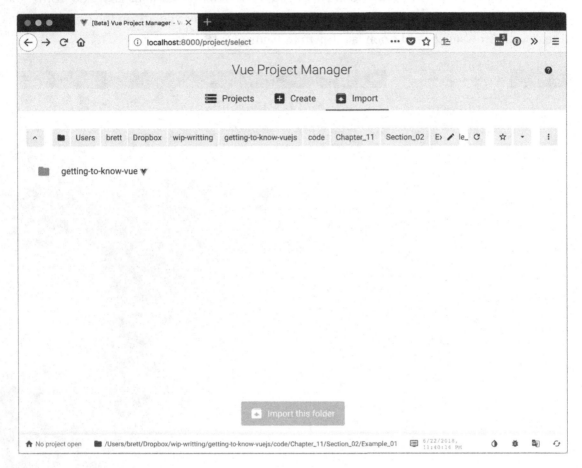

Figure 11-16. *Browsing to an existing Vue project*

Once we get to the project's root folder, the Import This Folder button will change to a darker green, which means we can start looking at the project in the UI.

The first screen, shown Figure 11-17, will show the plugins installed in the project.

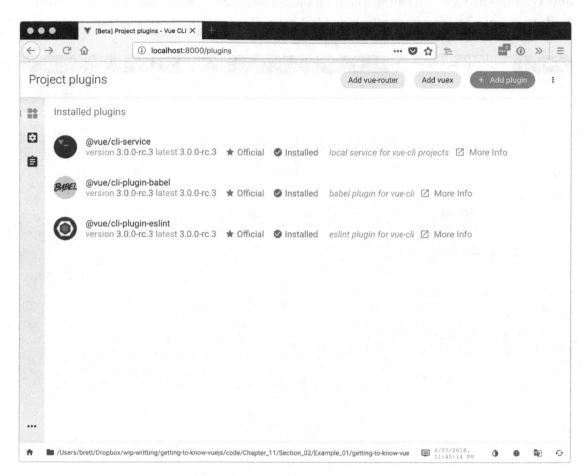

Figure 11-17. *Displaying the current project's plugins*

At the top of the plugins screen, you can choose to add plugins like the Vue Router and Vuex plugins. Or you can search for a plugin using the + `Add plugin` button, which leads to the plugin search screen shown in Figure 11-18.

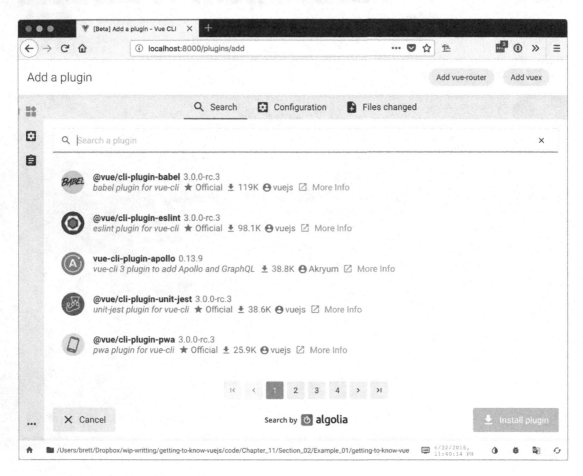

Figure 11-18. *Plugin search screen*

On the left side of the screen, we can choose to look at the project configuration with the Gear icon. In Figure 11-19, we can view the options for the Vue CLI.

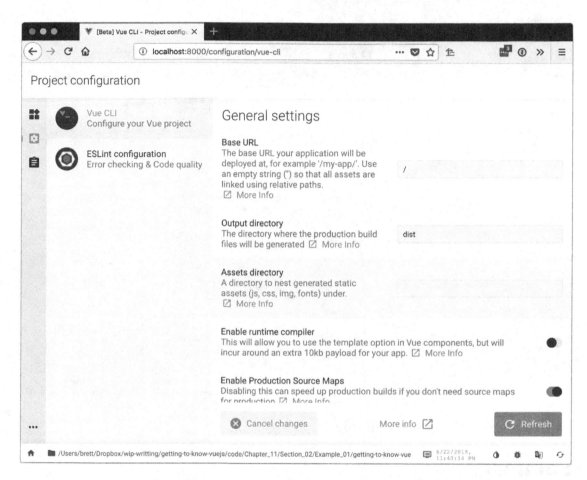

Figure 11-19. *Looking through the configuration options for the Vue CLI*

The third option on the left menu is the project tasks. We can see that these are the build-type tasks that we ran from the command line in Figure 11-20. We can now run them from the UI.

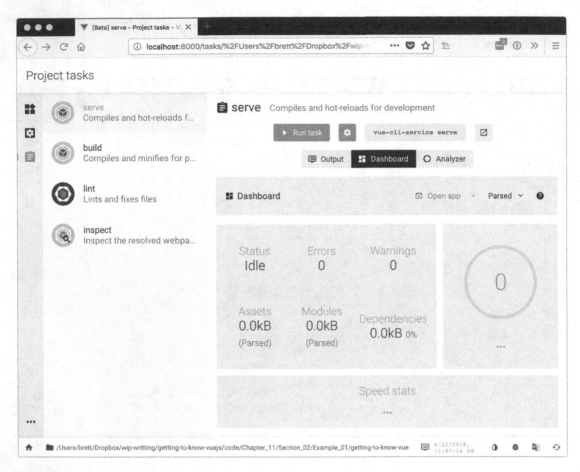

Figure 11-20. *Project tasks display*

Summary

In this chapter we learned about single file components (SFCs) and the Vue CLI. These two tools work together to create a more seamless development environment with access to more advanced techniques like transpiling and preprocessors.

CHAPTER 12

Using Routers

Being able to quickly change the look and layout of a page without doing a full-page refresh is awesome, but users like to have links that take them directly to content as well. After all, what good is a nice web app if you can't share a link to the content? This chapter looks at a few different ways to implement routing with Vue.

DIY Router

First up in our list of router options is the famous do-it-yourself (DIY) router. With the DIY router, you don't get any features to start with since you are creating it yourself. What you do get is possibly the lightest router option. If you don't need anything more than to change between pages, this may be your best option.

Setting Up the DIY Router

To get started with a DIY router, we will need some components. Listing 12-1 shows three components:

- `fourOhFour`: When a route isn't found
- `main`: For our default path
- `contactUs`: For our Contact Us page

The `main` and `contactUs` components are added to a `routes` object that has the path for each component as the name and the components as the values. The `fourOhFour` component will be used when the path isn't found in our `routes` object.

© Brett Nelson 2018
B. Nelson, *Getting to Know Vue.js*, https://doi.org/10.1007/978-1-4842-3781-6_12

Listing 12-1. Setting Up Our DIY Router Components

```
const fourOhFour = {
  data: function() {
    return {
      url: window.location.hash
    };
  },
  template: `
  <div>
    <p>Sorry, URL not found : {{url}} </p>
    <p>¯\\_(ツ)_/¯</p>
  </div>
  `
};

const main = {
  template: `
    <p>Welcome to <strong>Getting to Know Vue.js</strong></p>
  `
};
const contactUs = {
  template: `
    <p>Contact Us @ <strong>Getting to Know Vue.js</strong></p>
  `
};

const routes = {
  '#/': main,
  '#/contact-us': contactUs
};
```

In our app, we will add the routes to the `data` object with a value for the `currentPath` that we set to the `window.location.hash`. We also have a method that sets the value of `currentPath` to the hash of the target from the event and a computed property that returns the `currentView` from the `routes` based on the current path or on our `fourOhFour` component.

We can see this set up—along with the template that uses the Vue is directive to dynamically set the component based on the currentView—in Listing 12-2.

Listing 12-2. Our DIY Router App

```
var app = new Vue({
  el: '#app',
  data: {
    currentPath: window.location.hash,
    routes: routes
  },
  methods: {
    navigate: function($event) {
      this.currentPath = $event.target.hash;
    }
  },
  computed: {
    currentView: function() {
      return this.routes[this.currentPath] || fourOhFour;
    }
  },
  template: `
    <div>
      <ul>
        <li>
          <a href="#/"
            v-on:click="navigate">
              Main
          </a>
        </li>
        <li>
          <a href="#/contact-us"
            v-on:click="navigate">
              Contact Us
          </a>
        </li>
```

```
    </ul>
    <div v-bind:is="currentView">
    </div>
  </div>
  `

});
```

If we look at our app in the browser, we will see Figure 12-1 when we first navigate to the app. Figure 12-2 shows the Contact Us page. Finally, Figure 12-3 shows the result if we enter the wrong URL.

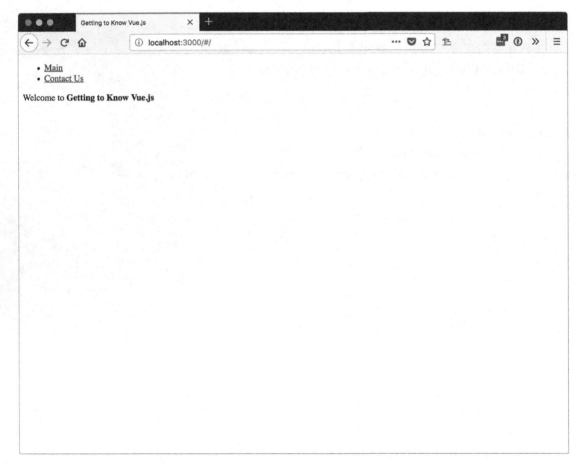

Figure 12-1. *Our DIY router displaying the main page*

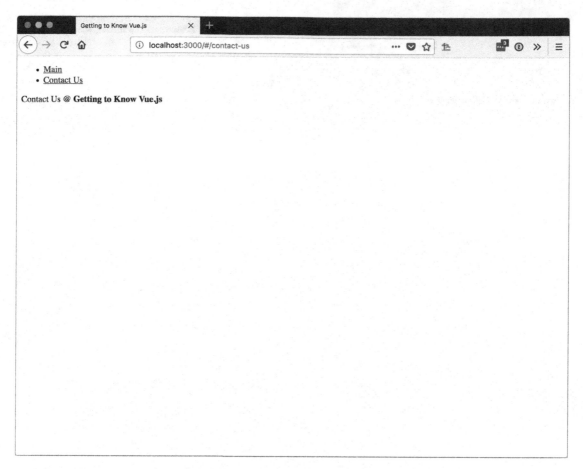

Figure 12-2. *Our DIY router displaying the Contact Us page*

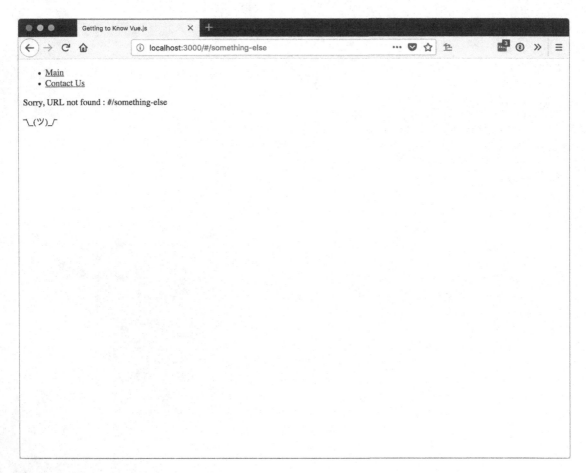

Figure 12-3. Our DIY router displaying the 404 page

Vue-Router

The Vue-Router is the official router of Vue. It integrates with Vue, thus allowing it to work more seamlessly with Vue. It has some nice features, such as nested routes, modular configuration, route parameters, query string parameters, and wildcard support, to name a few.

Setting Up Vue-Router

Vue-Router can be added to your project through NPM, if you are using a package manager, with the `npm install vue-router` command. Otherwise, you can add a reference to the CDN, as shown in Listing 12-3.

Listing 12-3. Referencing a CDN to Use Vue-Router

```
<script src="https://unpkg.com/vue-router/dist/vue-router.js"></script>
```

If you are using a module system, you will need to import Vue-Router into your app and call Vue.use on it, as shown in Listing 12-4.

Listing 12-4. Getting Vue-Router Ready Using a JavaScript Module System

```
import Vue from 'vue';
import Router from 'vue-router';

Vue.use(Router);
```

Note   The Vue.use(Router); command that we use here gets Vue ready to use the Vue-Router plugin. Later, we will configure a Vue-Router instance with routes that we will pass into our Vue instance, when we create it in Listing 12-6.

We use similar components that we defined for our DIY router in Listing 12-1, with the only big difference being that the fourOhFour component now uses the $router object to get the current path, as shown in Listing 12-5.

Listing 12-5. Our Updated FourOhFour Component Using the $router Object to Get the Current Path

```
const FourOhFour = {
  computed: {
    url: function() {
      return this.$router.currentRoute.path;
    }
  },
  template: `
<div>
    <p>Sorry, URL not found : {{url}} </p>
    <p>`\\_(ツ)_/`</p>
</div>
  `
};
```

The $router object is passed to the components from the parent Vue instance, which in our case is the app.

With Vue-Router added to our project and our component adjusted to use the $router, we need to create an array of routes before we can use them. Each route can have name, path, and should have a component. The component can be one that was defined previously or a Vue options object.

Our routes will look like Listing 12-6.

Listing 12-6. Creating Our Routes Array

```
const routes = [
  {
    path: '/',
    name: 'main',
    component: Main
  },
  {
    path: '/contact-us',
    name: 'contact-us',
    component: ContactUs
  },
  {
    path: '/*',
    name: 'notFound',
    component: FourOhFour
  }
];
```

If you are wondering about the last router that has the path of /*, that is our wildcard path and will show our FourOhFour component.

To create our router, we will call new VueRouter and pass in the routes. The routes can be passed in using JavaScript object destructuring or passed as objects that have a property named routes that is our array. Listing 12-7 shows both methods.

Listing 12-7. Creating Our Router

```
// Using JavaScript object destructuring
let router = new VueRouter({ routes });
// Using a JavaScript object with a parameter named 'routes'
let router = new VueRouter({ routes: routes });
```

Now all that's left is to use the router in our app and to add the `<router-view>` component to our app template. The `<router-view>` component was included in our project when we added the Vue-Router and is the same place where the router will insert the component for the current path.

Listing 12-8 shows our app adding the router and using the `<router-view>`. It also includes two `<router-links>`. The `<router-links>` were also included with the Vue-Router and can be used to navigate to new routes.

Listing 12-8. Our App Using the Vue-Router

```
var app = new Vue({
  router,
  el: '#app',
  template: `
    <div id="app">
      <div id="nav">
        <router-link
          to="/">
            Home
        </router-link> |
        <router-link
          to="/contact-us">
            Contact Us
        </router-link>
      </div>
      <router-view/>
    </div>
    `
});
```

When we first load our app, we should now see Figure 12-4. Figure 12-5 shows what it looks like now when we click on the Contact Us link. Figure 12-6 shows what happens if we go to any other URL.

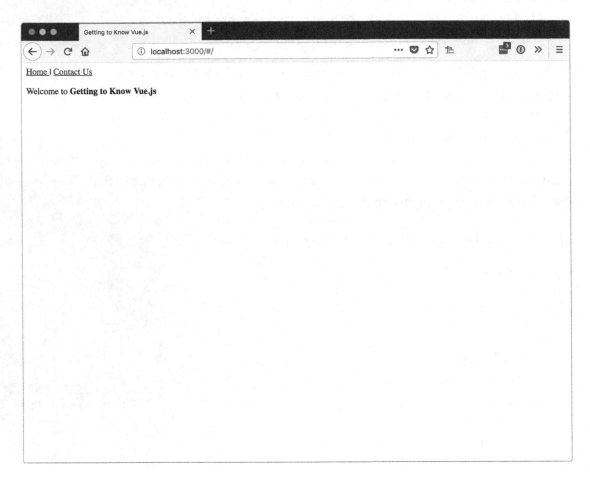

Figure 12-4. *Our Vue-Router main page*

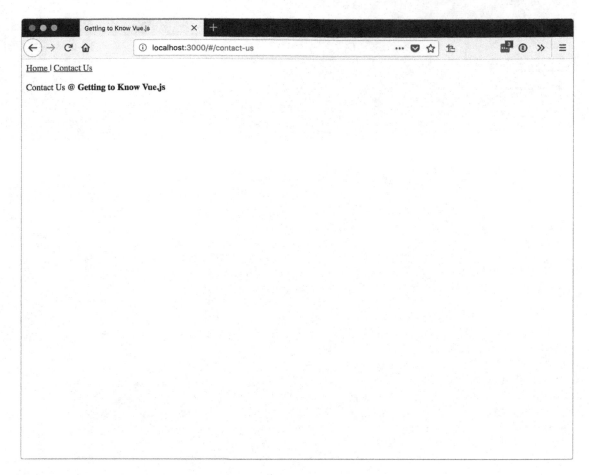

Figure 12-5. *Our Vue-Router Contact Us page*

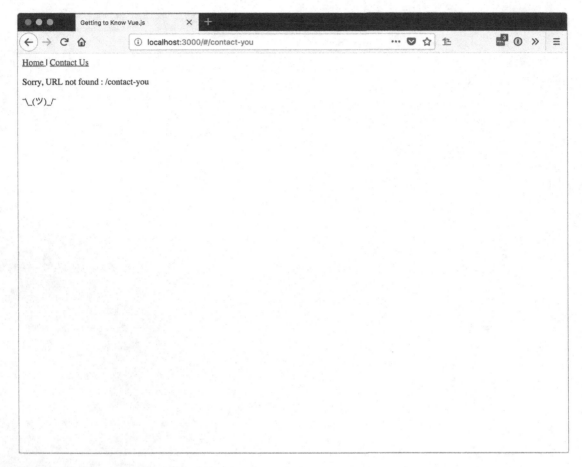

Figure 12-6. *Our Vue-Router 404 page*

Passing Parameters

One thing the Vue-Router can help us handle is pass parameters.

Route Parameters

We can define router parameters in the path for a route by starting a URL segment with a colon (:). Listing 12-9 shows a route for a profile. For the most part, it looks like the other routes we've had, with the main difference being that the path has two segments and the second segment starts with a colon. In case you are wondering, we will look at the component shortly.

Listing 12-9. Setting Up a Route to Accept a Parameter Named userName

```
{
  path: '/profile/:userName',
  name: 'profile',
  component: Profile
},
```

Now we need to create a link to this new path. To do that, we will add a new `<router-link>` in our app thats to attribute is set to `/profile/Getting to Know Vue.js`. This URL matches the path we defined in our router, with `/profile/` as the base for the path and `Getting to Know Vue.js` as the parameter named `userName`. Listing 12-10 shows the complete `<router-link>`.

Listing 12-10. Router Link Passing a Parameter

```
<router-link
  to="/profile/Getting to Know Vue.js">
    Profile
</router-link>
```

Now that we have a route defined with a parameter and a link that will take us there, we should take a look at the component that will handle this path.

Listing 12-11 shows our `Profile` component. The main thing to look at here is that we use the `$route` property to access the parameters. Since we are in the template, we don't have to use `this`. However, if we wanted to access the parameters in the JavaScript for the `Profile` component, we can do so by using `this.$route`. The `$route` object is a reference to the current active route.

Note   We can also access a reference to the router that we passed into our Vue app from our components with `this.$router`.

Listing 12-11. Profile Component Using $route to Access the username Parameter

```
const Profile = {
  template: `
    <p>
```

```
  User Name: <strong>
    {{ $route.params.userName }}
  </strong>
</p>
```

`};`

When we navigate to our profile page with `<router-link>`, we should see something like Figure 12-7.

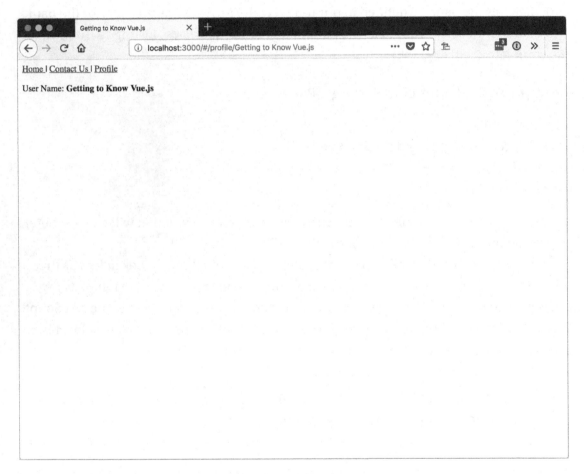

Figure 12-7. *Viewing our profile*

Passing Parameter Objects

It is possible to pass an object using the `<router-link>` to attribute with `v-bind`. In Listing 12-12, we use `v-bind` to navigate to the route named `profile` and pass the parameter named `user`. The `user` parameter has the `name` and `email` properties.

Listing 12-12. Using v-bind to Pass an Object to a Path

```
<router-link
  v-bind:to="{
    name : 'profile',
    params: { user: {
      name: 'Getting to Know Vue.js',
      email : 'gettingToKnowVuejs@Apress.com'
    }
  }
}">
  Profile
</router-link>
```

If we adjust our router to have `user` as the parameter and our `Profile` component to access the name and email from the `user` parameter, as shown in Listing 12-13, we can navigate to the profile page and see the results in Figure 12-8.

Listing 12-13. Accessing an Object Passed as a Route Parameter in a Component

```
const Profile = {
  template: `
    <div>
      <h3>User</h3>
      <p>
        Name: <strong>
              {{ $route.params.user.name }}
              </strong>
      </p>
```

```
    <p>
      Email: <strong>
                {{ $route.params.user.email }}
             </strong>
    </p>
  </div>
    `

};
```

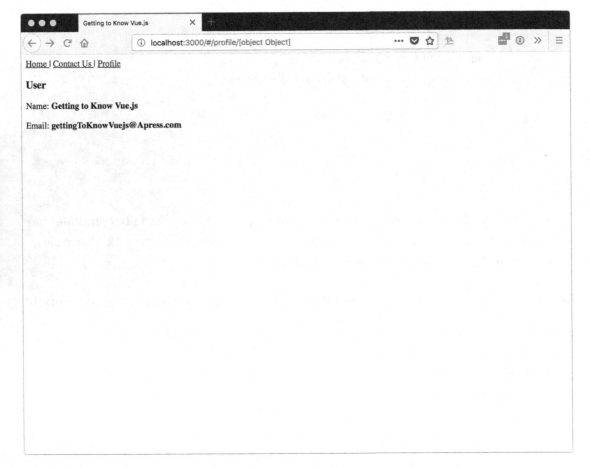

Figure 12-8. *Using an object as a route parameter*

You might have noticed in the URL that it now says /profile/[object object] and that doesn't look so good. We can change the route path so we don't pass the user object as a URL parameter by passing it to a property of the component.

Listing 12-14 is an update to our route for the profile. We remove the URL parameter and add a property name called props with a value of true. Using the props options with a value of true will pass any parameters we pass to the components properties. So now we just need to add a prop named user to our Profile component.

Listing 12-14. Using Props in the Route to Populate a Component's Properties

```
{
  path: '/profile/',
  name: 'profile',
  component: Profile,
  props: true
},
```

Next, we need to handle the props that are passed by the router. In Listing 12-15, we add a prop named user of type Object. In the template, we use this to access the name and email. These changes should result in our view looking like Figure 12-9 when we navigate to the profile page.

Listing 12-15. Using Props in Our Profile Component

```
const Profile = {
  props: {
    user: Object
  },
  template: `
    <div>
      <h3>User</h3>
      <p>
        Name: <strong>
                {{ user.name }}
              </strong>
      </p>
```

```
    <p>
      Email: <strong>
                {{ user.email }}
            </strong>
    </p>
  </div>
`

};
```

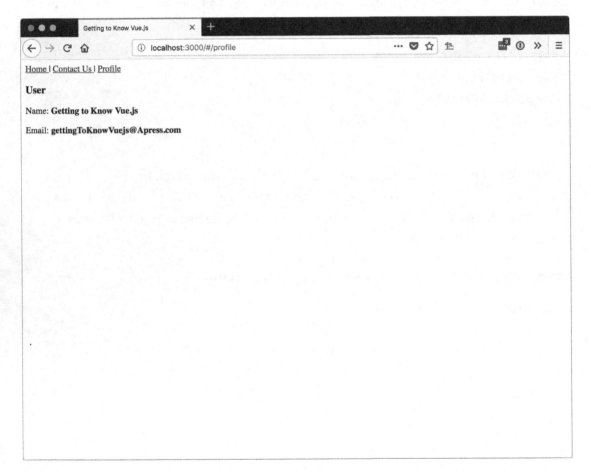

Figure 12-9. *Using the user property that was passed to the Profile component to get the name and email*

Navigating from JavaScript

We can use the router instance to push a new navigation event onto the stack. In Listing 12-16, we push the contact-us path onto the router.

Listing 12-16. Pushing a New Route Onto the Router

```
goToContactUs: function() {
  this.$router.push('contact-us');
}
```

This is the same as pushing an object with a property named path defined as contact-us, as shown in Listing 12-17.

Listing 12-17. Pushing an Object that Defines the Path Onto the Router

```
goToContactUs: function() {
  this.$router.push({ path: 'contact-us' });
},
```

We can also navigate by passing an object that defines the name of the path we want to go to. Listing 12-18 shows the process of pushing a named path to the router.

Listing 12-18. Pushing a Router Object that Defines the Name of the Route

```
goToContactUs: function() {
  this.$router.push({ name: 'contact-us' });
},
```

We can also push a new route with parameters. Listing 12-19 navigates to the profile page by passing the same values we used with the <router-link> previously.

Listing 12-19. Passing Parameters While Navigating in JavaScript

```
goToContactUs3: function() {
  this.$router.push({
    name: 'profile',
    params: {
      user: {
```

```
        name: 'Getting to Know Vue.js',
        email: 'gettingToKnowVuejs@Apress.com'
      }
    }
  });
}
```

Redirects

We can also define redirects in our router. *Redirects* allow us to move users to new content or updated URLs if we change the paths.

To define a redirect, we add a new route. It contains the `path` property, which is defined as the route we want to redirect, and a `redirect` property, which is the new target URL. Listing 12-20 shows a redirect of /home to /.

Listing 12-20. Adding a Redirect Route

```
{
  path: '/home',
  redirect: '/'
},
```

Aliases

Similar to redirects, aliases take the URL path to a different target, but instead of moving the user to a new URL, they keep users on the same path they navigated to and show the components from the defined route.

In Listing 12-21 we add an alias to our main route definition. Figure 12-10 shows our Main component when we now navigate to the /main URL path.

Listing 12-21. Adding an Alias to Our Main Route

```
{
  path: '/',
  name: 'main',
  alias: '/main',
  component: Main
},
```

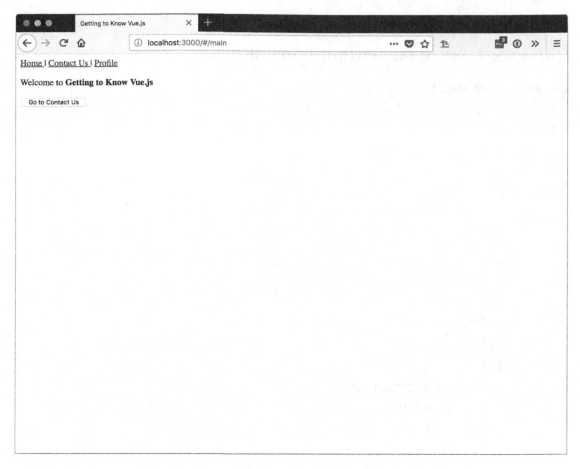

Figure 12-10. *Viewing the main component with the main alias*

The Page.js Router

The official Vue-Router isn't the only router out there. We can set up our Vue app to work with Page.js as well.

Page.js is a lightweight client-side router based on the router pattern used with Express. This pattern might be more comfortable for some.

To use the Page.js router, we will use the same components from Listing 12-1. Our app will be a little different, as we won't be doing any work in the app to handle the route and we will have the currentView be a data property instead of a computed property. This way, we can set it from outside the app.

Listing 12-22 shows our new app, all set up.

Listing 12-22. Setting Our App Up to Work with Page.js

```
var app = new Vue({
  el: '#app',
  data: {
    currentView: { template: '<p>Please Wait...</p>' }
  },
  template: `
    <div>
      <ul>
        <li>
          <a href="/" >
              Main
          </a>
        </li>
        <li>
          <a href="/contact-us" >
              Contact Us
          </a>
        </li>
      </ul>
      <div v-bind:is="currentView">
      </div>
    </div>
    `
});
```

You can see that we are setting the value of currentView to a Vue options object that has a template that says <p>Please wait..</p> This will be replaced once the router loads the current path.

We need to include a reference to the Page.js library. So we should add the reference to the CDN from Listing 12-23 to our HTML page.

Listing 12-23. Adding the Page.js Reference

```
<script src="https://cdn.rawgit.com/visionmedia/page.js/master/page.js">
</script>
```

All that's left now is to set up Page.js to work with Vue.

After the Vue app is created in our app.js, let's set up our routes.

Each route will take the path the route is for and the function to perform when the route happens. We are setting these routes up after the Vue app so we can use the reference to the app and set currentView.

For each route we will set the currentView to the component that we want to use. Listing 12-24 shows our complete route, all set up and calling page() to get things working.

Listing 12-24. Setting Up the Page.js Routes

```
page('/', function() {
  app.currentView = main;
});
page('/contact-us', function() {
  app.currentView = contactUs;
});
page('*', function() {
  app.currentView = fourOhFour;
});
page();
```

This will give us enough routing that, when we load the page in the browser, we should see Figure 12-11 on the first page load. Likewise, Figure 12-12 shows what we see when we select the Contact Us link.

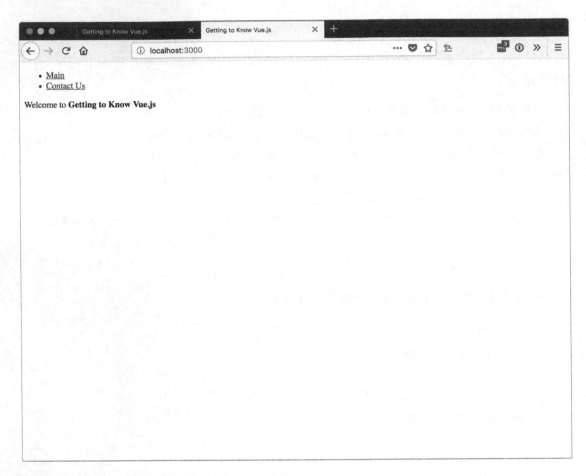

Figure 12-11. *First page load with Page.js*

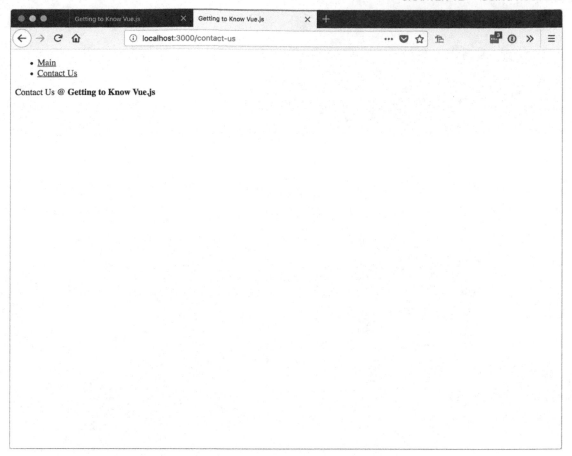

Figure 12-12. *Navigating to the Contact Us page with Page.js*

Summary

In this chapter we learned about routers. Creating your own router can be an option if you are looking for something that is lightweight and you don't mind doing all the work yourself. Vue-Router provides us with a full-feature approach to routing with options to pass data via URL parameters or directly to component props. We also saw that it's possible to use routers provided by other open source projects with Vue.

Index

© Brett Nelson 2018
B. Nelson, *Getting to Know Vue.js*, https://doi.org/10.1007/978-1-4842-3781-6

W, X, Y, Z